W9-APT-333

The Family Therapy Collections

James C. Hansen, Series Editor

Jill Elka Harkaway, Volume Editor

EATING DISORDERS

AN ASPEN PUBLICATION®
Aspen Publishers, Inc.
Rockville, Maryland
Royal Tunbridge Wells
1987

Library of Congress Cataloging in Publication Data

Eating disorders.

(The Family Therapy Collections; 20)
"An Aspen publication."
Includes bibliographies and index.
1. Eating disorders — Treatment. 2. Family psychotherapy. I. Harkaway, Jill Elka. II. Series.
[DNLM: 1. Appetite Disorders — therapy. 2. Family Therapy.
W1 FA454N v.20 / WM 175 E146]
RC552.E18E28   1987   616.3   86–26572
ISBN: 0-89443-619-8

The Family Therapy Collections series is indexed in *Psychological Abstracts* and the PsycINFO database

Copyright © 1987 by Aspen Publishers, Inc.
All rights reserved.

Article reprints are available from University Microfilms International,
300 North Zeeb Road, Dept. A.R.S., Ann Arbor, MI 48106.

Aspen Publishers, Inc. grants permission for photocopying for personal or internal use,
or for the personal or internal use of specific clients registered with the Copyright
Clearance Center (CCC). This consent is given on the condition that the copier pay a
$1.00 fee plus $.12 per page for each photocopy through the CCC for photocopying
beyond that permitted by the U.S. Copyright Law. The fee should be paid directly to the
CCC, 21 Congress St., Salem, Massachusetts 01970.
0–89443–619–8/87 $1.00 + .12.

This consent does not extend to other kinds of copying, such as copying for general
distribution, for advertising or promotional purposes, for creating new collective works,
or for resale. For information, address Aspen Publishers, Inc.,
1600 Research Boulevard, Rockville, Maryland 20850.

Editorial Services: Ruth Bloom

Library of Congress Catalog Card Number: 86–26572
ISBN: 0-89443-619-8
ISSN: 0735-9152

Printed in the United States of America

1   2   3   4   5

Table
of
Contents

Board
of
Editors

Editor
JAMES C. HANSEN
State University of New York at Buffalo
Buffalo, New York

JAMES F. ALEXANDER
University of Utah
Salt Lake City, Utah

CAROLYN L. ATTNEAVE
University of Washington
Seattle, Washington

JOHN ELDERKIN BELL
Stanford University
Palo Alto, California

EVAN IMBER-BLACK
University of Calgary
Calgary, Alberta, Canada

STEVE DESHAZER
Brief Family Therapy Center
Milwaukee, Wisconsin

HOLLIS A. EDWARDS
Toronto East General Hospital
Toronto Family Therapy Institute
Toronto, Ontario, Canada

NATHAN B. EPSTEIN
Brown University
Butler Hospital
Providence, Rhode Island

CRAIG A. EVERETT
Florida State University
Tallahassee, Florida

CELIA JAES FALICOV
University of California
Medical School
San Diego, California

DAVID A. FREEMAN
University of British Columbia
Vancouver, B.C., Canada

ALAN S. GURMAN
University of Wisconsin
Medical School
Madison, Wisconsin

PAULETTE MOORE HINES
Rutgers Medical School
New Brunswick, New Jersey

ALAN J. HOVESTADT
East Texas State University
Commerce, Texas

JOHN HOWELLS
Institute of Family Psychiatry
Ipswich, England

DAVID KANTOR
Kantor Family Institute
Cambridge, Massachusetts

Board of Editors
continued

FLORENCE W. KASLOW
Kaslow Associates, P.A.
West Palm Beach, Florida

DAVID P. KNISKERN
University of Cincinnati
College of Medicine
Central Psychiatric Clinic
Cincinnati, Ohio

LUCIANO L'ABATE
Georgia State University
Atlanta, Georgia

JUDITH LANDAU-STANTON
University of Rochester
Medical Center
Rochester, New York

KITTY LAPERRIERE
Ackerman Institute for Family Therapy
Columbia University
School of Medicine
New York, New York

HOWARD A. LIDDLE
University of California at San Francisco
School of Medicine
San Francisco, California
    and
Family Institute of San Francisco
San Francisco, California

ARTHUR MANDELBAUM
The Menninger Foundation
Topeka, Kansas

BRAULIO MONTALVO
Philadelphia Child Guidance Clinic
Philadelphia, Pennsylvania

AUGUSTUS Y. NAPIER
The Family Workshop
Atlanta, Georgia

DAVID H. OLSON
University of Minnesota
St. Paul, Minnesota

VIRGINIA M. SATIR
ANTERRA, Inc.
Menlo Park, California

RICHARD C. SCHWARTZ
Institute of Juvenile Research
Chicago, Illinois

RODNEY J. SHAPIRO
Veterans Administration
Medical Center
San Francisco, California

JUDITH S. WALLERSTEIN
Center for the Family in Transition
Corte Madera, California

FROMA WALSH
University of Chicago
Chicago, Illinois

CARL A. WHITAKER
University of Wisconsin-Madison
Madison, Wisconsin

ROBERT HENLEY WOODY
University of Nebraska at Omaha
Omaha, Nebraska

Series Preface

THE *FAMILY THERAPY COLLECtions* is a quarterly publication in which topics of current and specific interest to family therapists are presented. Each volume contains articles authored by practicing professionals, providing in-depth coverage of a single aspect of family therapy. This volume focuses on eating disorders.

Many people experience problems with weight control. The concerns vary from an inability to maintain a proper diet to starvation. These concerns and behaviors include distorted beliefs and attitudes about food, weight, and body shape. These values, beliefs, and attitudes are interrelated with family characteristics. Therefore, family therapy has become a major treatment mode for eating disorders. For many years anorexia nervosa was the eating disorder that received the primary focus. In recent years bulimia and obesity have been recognized as major eating disorders. This volume will cover all three problems and a variety of treatment approaches.

Family therapists are seeing an increasing number of persons with eating disorders and need a conceptual framework to guide the assessment of the individual and family and to plan treatment. Although family therapy is a major approach in treating eating disorders, therapists use a broad range of interventions. The authors recognize the complexity of eating disorders and present several models and contents for treatment. A significant aspect of this volume is the practical nature of the articles. The articles present case illustrations, descriptions of techniques and meaningful ideas for family therapists.

Jill Harkaway, EdD, is the volume editor. She is an Assistant Professor and Psychologist in the Departments of Psychiatry and Pediatrics at Tufts Medical School, New England Medical Center. She is a family therapist and co-director of the Obesity Clinic. Dr. Harkaway is also co-director of the Greater Lawrence Training Institute, a training program in Milan Systemic Therapy. She serves on the editorial board of the *Journal of Marital and Family Therapy*. For the past seven years she has conducted research and provided clinical treatment focusing on obesity. Dr. Harkaway has developed a meaningful organization for the topic of eating disorders and selected outstanding family therapists to write articles illustrating their specialties.

James C. Hansen
Series Editor

Preface

E ATING DISORDERS PRESENT a fascinating cybernetic problem. Perhaps more than any other symptom, they reflect the complexity and interrelationships of multiple factors: biological, genetic, psychological, behavioral, environmental, systemic, ethnic, and sociological. Unfortunately, the same rich complexity which makes the study of eating disorders so intriguing also makes clinical treatment extremely difficult. This difficulty is exacerbated by the lack of a tradition of treatment. Bulimia has only recently achieved status as a psychiatric syndrome (DSM III, 1980). Anorexia nervosa has become a serious concern only within the last twenty years. Obesity, although it possesses a long history of research and treatment, continues to defy attempted solutions.

An interesting historic relationship exists between eating disorders and family therapy. The work of Minuchin and his colleagues (1978) on anorexia has been extremely significant for both family therapy and the treatment of eating disorders. In many traditional psychiatric communities, Minuchin's work has given credibility to family therapy as an effective and legitimate treatment modality. Consequently, most treatment programs for anorexia include a family therapy component today.

Conversely, it was work with anorexia that shifted Selvini-Palazolli's thinking from a psychodynamic/individual model to a systemic/family model of treatment (1974), a shift which has had significance for the field of family therapy. Thus, work by family therapists has had impact on the field of eating disorders, and the work on eating disorders has had impact on family therapy.

This volume will acquaint the reader with the current state of family therapy treatment for eating disorders. It brings together exciting and innovative work by clinicians and researchers representing a variety of theoretical and clinical models. It covers not only bulimia and anorexia, but also obesity, a problem rarely included in publications on eating disorders. A variety of family therapy models is represented: structural, strategic, Milan systemic, transgenerational, experiential, cybernetic; and a variety of contexts: the individual, the couple, the family, the residential/peer system, and the larger societal system. Furthermore, each model has been developed to meet the needs of specific settings and patient populations.

The first five chapters explore theory and treatment of bulimia. Roberto is the Director of an Eating Disorder program which has family therapy as its primary mode of intervention, but also incorporates medical intervention, nutritional counseling, and hospitalization. In this chapter she presents her transgenerational family therapy model for the treatment of bulimia.

The Intensive Treatment Program for Bulimia is a multi-disciplinary intensive residential treatment program. Wooley, the Director of the program, and Lewis, the family therapist, describe the family therapy component of their program, a two-day multi-family "session" based on an experiential family therapy model.

Barrett and Schwartz have been conducting research on bulimia and family therapy for the past six years, and have been among the first family therapists to publish in this area. They present a Structural/Strategic family therapy model for the treatment of bulimia within the context of the couple relationship.

Moley, Director of the Eating Disorder Center of the Mental Research Institute, applies the Brief Therapy Model to the treatment of bulimia, as well as anorexia and compulsive eating. In this chapter he presents an analysis and treatment in terms of three levels of the system: the individual, the interpersonal, and the societal.

Although bulimia is a major problem on college campuses, little work has been done on developing systemic treatment for this population. Terry presents a model for treatment based on an interactional/developmental approach, which makes use of the "obstacles" and intervenes in three contexts: individual, family, and residential/peer group.

The next three chapters address the treatment of obesity. McVoy, Director of the Eating Disorders Program at St. Albans Psychiatric Hospital, addresses the need for family therapy and an integrated treatment approach for obesity. He describes his program which is based on a family therapy model which integrates structural, strategic, and Bowenian models, and incorporates group therapy, nutritional counseling, and physical activity groups.

Keeney and the doctoral students with whom he worked at Texas Tech University report on their research project which applied cybernetic theory to the problem of weight control. In distancing themselves from pre-existing theories of etiology and pathology, they developed an innovative format for intervention.

Harkaway describes the treatment model she has developed within a pediatric obesity clinic based on Milan systemic therapy and incorporating medical and nutritional components. She explains the triage model they have developed and the assessment format.

The last two chapters address the treatment of anorexia. Sargent, Director of the Eating Disorder program at Philadelphia Child Guidance Clinic, has many years of clinical and research experience in family therapy of anorexia, and is widely published on this topic. He discusses the importance of integrating individual and family therapy as the most useful treatment approach.

Lastly, White, who works with many anorexic families in Australia, presents an analysis of anorexia based on cybernetic theory which addresses multiple levels of context. He presents principles and examples for interviewing and intervening which are consistent with cybernetic approach.

Although there are significant differences in the way these authors conceptualize the problem and in their style of intervention, there are many similarities. These similarities reflect the following salient issues in the field:

1. There is no one diagnostic "type" of eating disorder client system. Although there are certain patterns, there is also a diversity of family styles and characteristics.
2. Because of this diversity, there is an acknowledgment that treatment, if it is to be effective, must meet the idiosyncratic needs of the client system. Although the authors attempt to describe patterns, they are also careful not to be blinded by them. Therefore, there is no protocol for family therapy of eating disorders in this volume. It is the system that is treated, not the symptom.
3. There is a shift from the rigid definition of family as context to a more flexible definition of the significant system. Most authors agree that eating disorders are symptoms that occur on multiple levels of context simultaneously. The focus of intervention, as defined in this volume, represents a broad range, with many authors addressing more than one level concurrently or consecutively in their therapy. Attention is paid to all levels of context, ranging from the individual to the society, and to the relationships between levels.
4. There is an awareness of the physiological component and the importance and necessity of combining

family therapy with medical and physiological treatment.
5. Lastly, most of us working with eating disorders find ourselves as influenced and changed by the work as are the client systems. Many clinicians, like Selvini, start off working with one model, only to learn its limitations and begin to challenge working assumptions. Many of the authors in this volume have altered their practice in response to their treatment experience with eating disorders. Some integrate aspects of other family therapy models into their work, some integrate other treatment modalities such as group or individual therapy. It seems to me that this is the most systemic of processes, the ability to respond to the feedback from interventions by adapting to the particular system. In this way I see clinical work with eating disorders as a co-evolutionary process: the client system and the treatment system involved in a mutually influencing and helpful interaction. Perhaps that is part of its appeal to family therapists.

Jill Elka Harkaway
Volume Editor

REFERENCES

American Psychiatric Association. (1980). *Diagnostic and statistical manual of mental disorders* (3rd ed.). Washington, DC.

Minuchin, S., Rosman, B., & Baker, L. (1978). *Psychosomatic families: Anorexia Nervosa in context*. Cambridge, MA: Harvard University Press.

Selvini-Palazolli, M. (1974). *Self-starvation: from the individual to family therapy in the treatment of anorexia nervosa*. London: Chaucer.

1

Bulimia: Transgenerational Family Therapy

Laura Giat Roberto, PsyD
Director
Eating Disorders Program
Eastern Virginia Medical School and
  Senior Faculty
Eastern Virginia Family Therapy
  Institute
Virginia Beach, Virginia

SINCE THE FIRST PUBLICA-tions on family therapy for eating disorders appeared (Liebman, Minuchin, & Baker, 1974; Minuchin, Rosman, & Baker, 1978; Selvini-Palazzoli, Boscolo, Cecchin, & Prata, 1978), a plethora of models and strategies to treat these bizarre and potentially lethal disorders has evolved. Most of these models and treatment strategies are essentially symptom-focused. They address the family's current transactions around the binge-eating, self-induced emesis, laxative and diuretic abuse, and associated behavior of the identified patient (e.g., stealing, sexual promiscuity, alcohol and drug abuse, depression, fasting behavior). Perhaps this symptom focus reflects the high level of concern that most therapists experience regarding the medically and emotionally devastating effects of unchecked bulimia; for example, tooth loss and gum disease, menstrual irregularities, functional hypoglycemia, esophogeal tears, hiatal hernia, hypokalemia, dehydration, and cardiac arrest (Boskind-White & White, 1983).

Despite the necessity of direct, timely intervention in these destructive behaviors, the transgenerational model of therapy suggests that symptoms are too deeply rooted in familial belief systems and familial organization, and will not be modified in the long term unless those belief systems are also modified. The general rate of relapse in the treatment of eating disorders attests to a low success rate over the long term (Garfinkel &

Note: The author would like to acknowledge Robert Marshall Smith, LCSW, for his clinical participation on several cases; the staff of the Eating Disorders Program for their treatment commentaries; and Janet Smyer for her excellent typing.

Garner, 1982). In order to forestall relapse, the entire understructure of interactions and ascribed meanings in the extended family system must be changed.

The theory behind a transgenerational formulation of bulimia will be presented, with discussion of the processes by which values, roles, beliefs and mandates are transmitted over long time periods to the bulimic patient. Unique organizational and dynamic characteristics of bulimic families will be reviewed, with an emphasis not only on well-known interaction patterns *but also on the covert themes, beliefs, and world views supporting and perpetuating their interaction patterns*. A multidisciplinary team approach is required for both inpatient and outpatient programs of care (Roberto, 1986). In our program, for example, we will not provide outpatient family therapy for bulimia without ongoing follow-up by a specialist in internal medicine and a nutritionist who provides calorie-controlled meal plans on a 3 meals:2 snacks ratio. These adjuncts are necessary to ensure eradication of fasting-induced binges and to prevent electrolyte imbalance. Hospitalization is used in early phase treatment when purging occurs several times daily to prevent cardiac complications and death. In addition, many bulimic patients have a history of drug and/or alcohol abuse, as well as sexual abuse. Psychological trauma induced by substance addiction or by molestation also influences us to consider early phase hospitalization.

THREE-GENERATIONAL MODEL OF BULIMIA

Bulimia arises most commonly in middle to late adolescence and early adulthood.

Many patients report the onset of self-induced bingeing and purging in their late 20s and early 30s, but a careful eating disorders history generally reveals that these patients have had previous incidences of self-starvation, compulsive eating, and/or purging in adolescence, thus making the latest onset of symptoms technically a relapse. Family theorists have noted the developmental implications of this age-related disorder, namely, the inability of the family organization to tolerate and adapt to the separation, autonomy, and launching of the young adult offspring (Schwartz, Barrett, & Saba, 1985). A purely developmental perspective lacks specificity regarding the unique history of bulimic families and the emergence of the peculiar bingeing and purging rituals in adolescence, however.

Selvini-Palazzoli and her colleagues (Selvini-Palazzoli et al., 1978) noted that weight obsession, weight control, and purging occur in a family system that is rigidly impermeable to the outside world and internally extremely fluid with few boundaries. They described the offspring as inducted into a "three-way marriage" with the parents. This three-way marriage also exists in the grandparental generation, with one parent (usually the mother) having been similarly inducted. Thus, the loyalty bonds between at least one parent and his or her family of origin lead to a three-generational bond in which each offspring attends to the needs of his or her parents, to be attended to in turn by his or her offspring . . . and so on.

Melanie, a 36-year-old wife and mother, had been bingeing and purging three times a day for 18 years—

since the age of 18. From a large, devout Catholic family, she had obeyed her father and comforted her meek mother as "the good child" throughout her childhood and adolescence. This had necessitated some self-sacrifice, including refusal to tell her parents about her sexual abuse by an older brother for fear it would shock and hurt her overworked, unhappy mother. The parents maintained their marriage through strict religious observance and focus on the management of their six children.

At 18, Melanie married Thomas, a hard-working, authoritative man like her father. She continued to devote most of her thoughts and energies to the health and well-being of her mother, when she was not busy pleasing and obeying her husband. She began fasting to "stay slender for Tom," which led to bingeing, anxiety, and purging. The couple had two boys, Tom Junior and Steven. Tom Junior, the elder of the two boys, was quite devoted to his mother, feared for her health, and spent much of his free time helping her with housework, talking with her, and monitoring her food intake. He was socially withdrawn, self-critical, and overweight.

When the offspring of a family that is internally fluid and externally closed marries someone from a similarly organized family, the marriage may come to resemble the (symmetrical) marriage of siblings who are in positions of son or daughter to the parents first and husband or wife to each other second. If the offspring chooses a partner who, because he or she was separated and launched early, is bereft of extended family involvement, the partner may maintain a (complementary) position of authoritative parent first and spouse second (McVoy, 1984). In this second generation of the three-generation model, many issues arise concerning success and stability of the family. In the first type of marriage, successes are intended to please and gratify the families of origin; in the second type of marriage, these achievements are intended to replicate or replace the lost extended family interconnections.

As a result of the emphasis on success and security, these spouses feel shame and guilt in the event of real or imagined financial and social failures. Generally, the husband holds himself responsible for financial success and stability, while the wife often takes on the role of producer of social success and a second concern—physical attractiveness and fitness. Many families spend hours of therapy time describing their lack of confidence because the husband has failed in independent business, has not provided income to his parents, or has not advanced on the ladder of promotion quickly. Similarly, wives often show embarrassment if they do not cook nutritious meals nightly, fail to retain a slim and fashionable figure after the birth of children, or are not involved in community work. Thus, the second generation in these families feels pressures to extend or replace the interconnectedness of the first generation.

Into this pressured "sibling" or "parental" marriage come children, the third generation of the model. Generally, they are "good" children in that they grow up without severe delinquent, antisocial, impulsive, or running away behavior. This observation is consistent with the fact that, in centripetal, internally fluid families avoidant of extrafamilial connections, children are bound early on emotional and cognitive levels to value and respond to the needs of the parents *within* the home by remaining overtly dependent.

As Stierlin (1972) described this binding process, the first emphasis is placed on ensuring security within the home and closing out an external world that is perceived as dangerous and/or hostile. Over time, the selected child becomes infantilized. Either one or both parents are exceedingly generous to the child, as well as intrusive on an emotional level. This overinvestment in the child may be a response to pressures experienced in highly connected families of origin or an attempt to counteract deprivations in familial connectedness for the parent(s). The overinvestment is also functional in that it forestalls a greater awareness of parental wishes that might threaten the cohesion of the nuclear family, such as dissatisfaction with marital intimacy or frustration with an overly complementary, "parental" marriage.

The entry of certain children into the marriage of their parents creates the "three-way marriage." In the "sibling" marriage, this triangulated child provides reassurance and nurturance to both parents. In the "parental" marriage, this child is usually allied with the parent perceived as stronger, or parental, but feels angry, guilty, and obligated toward the parent perceived as weaker, or infantilized (frequently, the mother).

The way in which index children are selected to enter into the parents' marriage by this transgenerational process is not yet fully understood. Statistically,

approximately 85% of our bulimic families have selected a daughter; only 15%, a son. Families, and the bulimic offspring, often reflect that the selected children have seemed especially devoted and responsive to the parents. Throughout middle childhood and preadolescence, these children "fit" the needs of the parents more and more closely, avoiding peer relationships, suppressing autonomous strivings, and controlling negative affect with depression, compulsive eating, substance abuse, and an obsessive focus on pleasing behaviors and weight. As time passes, they become increasingly unable to function outside the confines of the extended family. Finally, exposure to or experimentation with purging provides a final route for control of emotionality and external attractiveness.

UNIQUE CHARACTERISTICS OF BULIMIC FAMILIES

Loyalty and Obligation

The concept of filial loyalty has been discussed extensively by Nagy (Boszormenyi-Nagy & Ulrich, 1981). Intrafamilial loyalty in bulimic families appears to be responsible for many premature terminations and failures of treatment. Because the bulimic family member is so poorly individuated from her family of origin and spouse, and because she is clearly self-destructive and self-sacrificial in her symptoms, most therapists attempt early in treatment to encourage direct verbal expression of dissatisfactions, relationship problems, and individual needs or wishes. The immediate response to this encouragement is frequently increased purging, severe feelings of guilt, and even with-drawal from therapy (at the symptom bearer's request)!

There is an implicit demand for family cohesion, loyal behavior, and mutual protectiveness in bulimic families. Often, one member may appear to be exempt from the protection or loyalty of the others—frequently, the father or a highly involved grandparent. This exemption is more apparent than real, however, and if the therapist uses it to encourage direct expression of conflict, the symptoms-bearer's symptoms will escalate. Family members are usually unable to articulate this implicit loyalty-cohesion rule, but they express it as their perception that they are "a close and loving family." This curious behavior has also been observed in anorectic fami-lies (Selvini-Palazzoli, 1978; White, 1983). In our experience, the experien-tial "stickiness" generated by the demand for cohesion is equally operative in bulimia.

In addition to the loyalty-cohesion demands, family members usually feel a strong sense of obligation toward one another. Parental obligation includes concern that the children be provided for financially, given every social oppor-tunity, protected from every emotional or interpersonal hardship, and kept from failure experiences. Obligation in the offspring includes a determination to make the parents proud, attempts to in-crease their happiness, fear of disap-pointing them, and a desire to protect them from emotional loss (e.g., the loss ensuing if they should leave home for college).

Sally, a 17-year-old girl from a large, wealthy family, was the youngest daughter and the only one still resid-ing at home. Her father was fre-quently gone on business, leaving the mother alone save for Sally's companionship. Sally had been bulimic for 3 years, bingeing during the early morning hours while her parents slept and vomiting after each of the daily meals. She was slated for senior class valedictorian and had been Homecoming Queen. Only Sally's dance instructor had been told of the symptoms, since Sally felt that "my parents have given me every opportunity—none of my brothers or sisters has made prob-lems—it's my own fault I do this. It would kill my father; he's so proud of me. And my mother would be furious—she has so much on her mind already, the last thing she needs is to have to worry about me."

Success and Achievement

Most bulimic families have a tremendous drive for success. In American and Americanized families, success is often equated with monetary wealth (Schwartz et al., 1985). First- or second-generation immigrant families have different defini-tions of success, however. To them, success may involve maintenance of social status and influence in the church or community, or stability and security in a family home with well-behaved chil-dren and a satisfied husband.

Genograms of the extended bulimic family often show traumatic losses in previous generations, involving financial ruin, expatriation, separation from the nuclear family, chronic (treated or neglected) illness, and death. Surviving grandparents and young adults show a unique determination to compensate for, cover over, and overcome these losses at all costs. Discussion of this process may be considered embarrassing or even forbidden.

Fear of Conflict

In order to remain organized around three-generational bonds and to maintain cohesion, bulimic families have rigid taboos against sustained, direct disagreement and conflict. We do not mean to imply that conflict is not overt, as is the case with anorexic families (Minuchin et al., 1978). As the enmeshment between the bulimic offspring, her parents, and grandparents continues over time, bitter and explosive conflict can occur intermittently as she fails to fulfill familial expectations and instead turns to ritualistic bingeing and purging behavior. However, the conflicts are rarely directed toward the enmeshment and loyalty binds that create the tension. Rather, they are indirect and usually focus on demands that the bulimic stop purging, eat with the family, and improve her mood, or on other symptom-oriented communications.

In the bulimic family, conflict is not sustained long enough for resolution. The conflict reaches early closure through one of three means: (1) one of the participants becomes withdrawn or explosive, creating anxiety through the appearance of intense emotionality; (2) the conflict is conducted in a ritualistic, rote manner (as in a parental lecture) and draws to a ritualistic close; or (3) the bulimic member grows hopeless and leaves to binge and purge at the earliest opportunity. The bingeing and purging may be replaced by alcohol or drug abuse, for bulimic women are frequently cross-addicted.

Although the bulimic patient may report "getting upset" during familial conflict, the conflict is terminated early enough or is conducted carefully enough so that strong negative affect remains largely implicit. Anger, mistrust, frustration, and unpleasant assertions are never clearly articulated, for they would interrupt internally fluid boundaries within the family and instigate separation—with perceptions of loss. Guilt, concern, anxiety, shame, depression, and hopelessness are more likely to be expressed, as these affects support internally fluid boundaries, intensify perceptions of caring and involvement, and ensure mutual dependence and cohesion (Stierlin, 1972). Thus, the responses to conflict that emerge in bulimic families are not conducive to clarification of the family dysfunction, but instead obscure the peculiar implicit pressures in these families and even encourage further overinvolvement and conflict avoidance.

Jane, a 27-year-old wife who had been bingeing, vomiting, and abusing laxatives since adolescence, fought with her husband about only one thing: her flirtatiousness, which attracted men to her and caused her husband concern about her fidelity. The fights, instigated by her husband when Jane arrived home late from work or recreation, led Jane to complain that she was "confused, mixed up about myself, crazy, and having an identity crisis." These complaints, followed by days of purging, would lead her husband to protect, advise, and monitor her more closely, ensuring more involvement on his part and decreasing the chances of a marital breakup.

Weight, Fitness, and Physical Beauty

Perhaps the hallmark of the bulimic family, more so than for the anorexic family, is its intensive focus on controlling body weight and maintaining a healthy, attractive appearance. This preoccupation is equally likely to appear in male family members as in female family members. The parents may carry a mandate from the grandparents to avoid obesity and, subsequently, heart failure like grandfather or diabetes like grandmother. There may be concurrent athletic ambitions as, for example, in the "soccer family." These interests combine with the parents' investment in good nutrition, weight control, and their children's pleasing appearance. The children come to value these investments and attempt to personify them. Unfortunately, the success and achievement orientation of a bulimic daughter prevents her from ever feeling that she is pretty enough or has a sufficiently attractive figure.

THE FAMILY LEGACY: TOOL FOR CHANGE

All of the extended family characteristics and dominant beliefs reviewed earlier are of purely academic interest unless they can be utilized to produce symptom relief and, ultimately, change. In the process of treatment, the therapist reframes the dominant beliefs of the bulimic family in metaphorical terms. The reframings are used alternately to challenge and systematically address the bulimic family belief system in terms that seem familiar to the family members and are under therapeutic control. Because the reframings are couched in metaphorical, not technical, terms, they bring affective power

and drama into the rigid, emotionally constricted bulimic family system. Reframing and commenting on the dysfunctional belief system also matches the family's own experience, which is particularly historical and tradition-bound. Finally, because of the recurrent cycling of guilt and obligation among family members, metaphorical reframings are better tolerated in early sessions than are direct challenges. The primary method that we use for reframing transgenerational belief systems and linking them to the current bingeing and purging symptoms is the construction of the "family legacy."

A legacy refers to that which is handed down, like a gift, from one's ancestors. The unique beliefs, perceptions of the outside world, role expectations, and interaction patterns that have been described are the legacies of the bulimic family. One could think of these legacies as similar to "family myths." However, the term "myth" denotes unreality or legend, whereas the transgenerational patterns we observe seem desperately real to the affected families. Legacies then are actually systemic messages that family members transmit implicitly to each other about their most cherished traditions. They are perceived, responded to, and elaborated without ever being explicitly discussed, even during conflicts.

Although the family legacy is actually a systemic hypothesis that links bingeing and purging symptoms to dysfunctional family organization, there are two critical differences. First, the legacy always has a transgenerational, historical component, whereas systemic hypotheses may, but do not always, contain transgenerational information. Second, the themes, critical life events, and key words included in the family legacy come from specific beliefs, interactional patterns, and symptoms that are unique to the bulimic family. Otherwise, the constructed legacy is not isomorphic with the family's perceptions and fails to take into account the most crucial targets for change.

Therapeutically, the most effective way to enter the centripetal, constricted, psychosomatic, isolated organization of the bulimic family is through staged interventions around the family legacy. The model has three stages of treatment: constructing the family legacy (early phase); challenging the family legacy (midphase); and constructing alternatives (late phase therapy).

Constructing the Family Legacy

In working with legacies in a bulimic family, the therapist seeks to avoid an immediate focus on symptomatic behaviors (e.g., intrusiveness with the bulimic) and immediate challenge. Rather, the therapist moves to an intermediate position of reframing family behaviors, including the bulimic symptoms, as compliance with an underlying family legacy. The entire family is viewed as a symmetrical organization caught up in one relentless pursuit— preservation of their organization at all costs. It is essential in constructing the family legacy, as in formulating any systemic hypothesis, that every family member be included.

Initially, the therapist is accepting of "the facts of the situation" as the family presents them. With the family, including the extended family if at all possible, the therapist explores the bulimic's

symptoms, their chronicity, and spouse/family interventions that have been attempted. The therapist does not imply the existence of relationship problems, makes no inferences, and acknowledges the family's high level of concern, involvement, and emotional reactivity to one another.

Patterns in dominant beliefs and interactions are then assessed in terms of the three-generational family. The therapist inquires about somatic symptoms in others, acknowledged conflicts between the nuclear and extended family, family members who have been most proximal, and "mavericks" who have violated the family norms. The therapist then begins to make brief observations about intergenerational overinvolvement, oppressive interpersonal expectations, and the use of guilt or loyalty demands as motivators—again, without directly challenging them.

Finally, the therapist formulates a family legacy and delivers it to the family, marking the end of the early phase of treatment. When the bulimia is acute (less than 6 months' duration), the therapist may delay the delivery of the family legacy and attempt specific direct challenges (e.g., challenge of the coalition between a bulimic daughter and one parent against the other). Generally, this is not possible, however. With the delivery of the family legacy, the bulimic member is elevated from the status of ill victim to that of a dutiful, but doomed, child who is fulfilling the family legacy (Roberto, 1986).

Diane, a 28-year-old married woman with two children, had been married to Robert since high school graduation. She had not told Robert about her bingeing, laxative abuse, and vomiting during their courtship. Keeping destructive secrets was not a new or unusual thing for Diane, who had managed to hide her physical abuse by her mother from the four siblings who had lived at home throughout the period of abuse. Diane's siblings, six in all, had likewise withheld many frightening secrets from each other. A younger brother "hid" a gradual premorbid deterioration that culminated in a paranoid schizophrenic break. A sister "hid" her gay sexual preferences; while another sister compulsively overate in private.

Diane's parents protected the children and themselves from painful confrontations by maintaining a code of silence; eventually, the father disappeared entirely without explanation. The mother communicated with Diane and her siblings, even in their adulthood, only through fairy tales that she composed. Nothing whatsoever was known of the lives of Diane's grandparents, except that her maternal grandmother "lived on the wrong side of the tracks."

The legacy in this family was framed as group survival and mutual tolerance bought at the price of the secrets that family members withheld from each other (and themselves), even if it meant illness, depression, disappearance, and psychosis. In this context, Diane was declared to have found in bulimia a particularly effective method for containing her secrets and preventing their emergence, even with her own husband.

The family legacy is delivered as an empathic commendation of the family's attempts to ensure cohesion. This positive connotation immediately dilutes the guilt, obligation, and overinvestment characteristic of bulimic families. In addition, it positions the therapist to be allowed "into" the family, for he or she is not demanding change. Finally, it creates pressure in the form of a positive feedback loop; family members have been commended, but they are aware that their rigid family structure is producing a life-threatening illness.

Examples of constructed family legacies abound in published case studies of anorexia nervosa. Selvini-Palazzoli has described a family whose motto was "whoever separates himself from the family, is lost" (Selvini-Palazzoli et al, 1978). In the well-known case of structural family therapy, Minuchin (Aponte & Hoffman, 1973) used "the open [bedroom] door," symbolizing that the little daughters would never grow up and leave their lonely father. In the Kaplan family (Minuchin et al., 1978), he presented their legacy as "taking each other's voice." And in the Johnson family (White, 1983), the legacy (somewhat more specific) was that each second-born daughter would devote herself exclusively to her mother's needs. We have found that elements of affective power can be brought into these constricted families if the legacy contains specific references to points of change in the family's history, tragic losses, crises, disintegration of critical relationships, and other feared events. For example, one family in our program was told that their daughter Kathleen, "like her father, is determined to sacrifice and succeed in business, although she dislikes it and it alienates her mother, for she will never allow the family assets to be destroyed as they were when grandfather lived through the Depression.''

Challenging the Family Legacy

After the delivery of the family legacy, it is a small step to point out to the bulimic daughter and her family that they probably will not, and should not, suddenly shift from their tradition-bound and rigid belief system. The therapist binds the family by warning them more and more often of the consequences should they abandon their traditional structure and beliefs. The family therapy becomes a "sweat-box" where family members must repeatedly face the constricting, dehumanizing nature of their beliefs and behavior (Whitaker & Keith, 1981). Conflicts and symptoms are reframed to depict the bulimic family member as one who adheres to the family legacy. Her starvation, bingeing, and purging are described as self-sacrifice or extreme expressions of loyalty. Any crises (e.g., weight loss or persistent vomiting) that occur at this time are firmly tied to the family legacy.

Tension begins to increase during this phase of therapy as individual family members must decide whether to continue their previous behavior (with a growing awareness of its linkage to the bulimia) or to abandon the old structure for a new one that reflects current needs. The therapist does not engage in psychoeducation or give advice or reassurance. Rather, the therapist challenges the family members, often with humor, to give up their pursuit of success, their perfectionism, their demands for loyalty, and fear of conflict. The therapist implies that they do not have to change, but that only systemic change will eradicate the need for the bulimia.

The final challenge to the family is the prediction of the consequences of abandoning the bulimic family legacy. The therapist teases, encourages, and warns of dire repercussions for those whose beliefs differ from the old extended family beliefs and norms. Consequences in the extended family network include being disapproved of or disowned, losing security, or being cast adrift from one's past.

Constructing Alternatives

During the late phase of therapy, the therapist points out the practical consequences of abandoning the family legacy: parental divorce; depression in one or more members; loneliness; or the loss of an old, familiar, and comforting niche in the family. As the therapist "beats this dead horse," one family member is likely to demand change out of frustration and anxiety. At times, this is the bulimic daughter herself; she is often the most bound member of the system, however, and it is more commonly a peripheral or even extended family member who demands change. This pressure *from within the centripetal family system* shifts and curbs previous escalations and symptoms.

When pressure from within the family builds toward change, the therapist can change position and begin very tentatively to discuss alternative behavior. Casual assignments are used, ostensibly to test "how costly it will be to change." These assignments focus on behaviors that have supported the family legacy. For example, in the case of Kathleen, the parents were asked to leave their adult children at home and go spend money on marital recreation for one weekend. As the family tries new arrangements, the therapist warns, jokes, and sympathizes. Caution is required in giving and reviewing assignments, particularly successful ones. This therapist attitude has been aptly termed "guarded enthusiasm" (White, 1983). If the therapist responds very positively to signs of recovery, even in this late phase of therapy bulimic families may move together to exclude the outsider and return to their previous state of internal cohesion.

Finally, the old, centripetal family structure is challenged to its core by focusing gently, but firmly, on the boundaries between generations. Addressing *separately* the concerns of teen-agers, parents, and elders, the therapist reinforces their functional autonomy whenever possible. Interventions appear quite "structural" at the end of treatment, when the concept of being separated and different from one another is no longer threatening to the family members.

SUMMARY

Bulimia, with its deceptively mild veneer, desperate undercurrents, and dangerous medical complications, poses one of the most challenging and yet exciting problems that the family therapist is likely to see. Replete with crises on physiological, interpersonal, extended familial, and cultural levels, it is certainly one of the most complex of disorders. We believe that by looking beyond strictly focused symptom interventions, it is possible to mobilize tremendous change in what would seem to be severely constricted, tradition-bound, rigid, resistant and physically ill families. And, of course, producing tremendous change under those conditions attests to the unique power of family systems interventions.

REFERENCES

Boskind-White, M., & White, W. (1983). *Bulimarexia: The binge-purge cycle.* New York: W.W. Norton.

Garfinkel, P.E., & Garner, D.M. (1982). *Anorexia nervosa: A multidimensional perspective.* New York: Brunner/Mazel.

Liebman, R., Minuchin, S., & Baker L. (1974). The role of the family in the treatment of anorexia nervosa. *Journal of the American Academy of Child Psychiatry, 13,* 264–274.

McVoy, J. (1984). *Till death do us part: Treating the married anorexic.* Paper presented to the Annual Conference of Special Topics in Family Therapy, St. Albans Psychiatric Hospital, Radford, VA.

Minuchin, S., Rosman, B., & Baker, L. (1978). *Psychosomatic families: Anorexia nervosa in context.* Cambridge, MA: Harvard University Press.

Roberto, L.G. (1986). Bulimia: The transgenerational view. *Journal of Marital and Family Therapy, 12,* 231–240.

Schwartz, R.C., Barrett, M.J., & Saba, G. (1985). Family therapy of bulimia. In D.M. Garner & P.E. Garfinkel (Eds.), *Handbook of psychotherapy for anorexia nervosa and bulimia* (pp. 280–310). New York: Guilford Press.

Selvini-Palazzoli, M.S. (1978). *Self-starvation: From individual to family therapy in the treatment of anorexia nervosa.* New York: Jason Aronson.

Selvini-Palazzoli, M.S., Boscolo, L., Cecchin, G., & Prata, G. (1978). *Paradox and counterparadox.* New York: Jason Aronson.

Stierlin, H. (1972). *Separating parents and adolescents: A perspective on running away, schizophrenia, and waywardness.* New York: Quadrangle.

Whitaker, C.A., & Keith, D.V. (1981). Symbolic-experiential family therapy. In A.S. Gurman & D.P. Kniskern (Eds.), *Handbook of family therapy* (pp. 187–226). New York: Brunner/Mazel.

White, M. (1983). Anorexia nervosa: A transgenerational system perspective. *Family Process, 22,* 255–273.

2

Multi-Family Therapy within an Intensive Treatment Program for Bulimia

Susan C. Wooley, PhD
Director
Eating Disorders Clinic
Associate Professor
Psychiatry Department
University of Cincinnati Medical
  College
Cincinnati, Ohio
  and
Karen Gail Lewis, ACSW
Staff Therapist
Eating Disorders Clinic
Psychiatry Department
University of Cincinnati Medical
  College
Cincinnati, Ohio

When I pictured myself the thinnest I could be, I saw myself alone. It was lonely, but I didn't have to take care of anyone. And when I pictured myself the fattest I could be, there were lots of people around and I had to take care of them all.

• • •

Last night, Marie stole laxatives she said she didn't really want. The police caught her and called her mother. Today, she complains that her mother is too protective.

"Could you pretend you are your mother and talk about your life?" one of the therapists asks.

"About me or her?"

"About her. Say 'I'm Marie's mother . . . '"

"I'm Marie's mother. . . . I'm very worried about Marie. I know she's old enough to be an adult, but still I feel she needs a mother. . . . What else do I have to do in my life? I'm not very talented. I shouldn't be a substitute teacher because I don't have my degree and . . . I don't really know enough."

"Is your daughter smarter than you?" the therapist asks.

"A lot smarter than me. She's got a lot more opportunities, lots more than I ever had. . . . "

Based on a view of bulimia that emphasizes the problems of families in a period of rapid change in women's roles, the Intensive Treatment Program for Bulimia includes several forms of therapy (Wooley & Kearney-Cooke, 1986; Wooley & Wooley, 1985). Six to eight bulimic women are housed in a hotel apartment for 3 ½ weeks and are responsible for their own food preparation. The women participate in nearly 8 hours of therapy per day. The more than 100 patients who have been treated have ranged in age from 18 to 36, with an average age of 24. They have been bulimic for 1 to 24 years, with an average duration of illness of nearly 8 years. Family therapy occupies a central role in treatment, although its role cannot be separated from those of the other treatment components.

DEVELOPMENTAL ISSUES IN BULIMIA BODY AND IMAGE DISTURBANCE

Researchers and theorists (e.g., Chodorow, 1978; Gilligan, 1982) have outlined the important differences in the traditional early childhood development of boys and girls. Boys' development has been marked by autonomous achievement, competition, and detachment, while girls have been raised to develop values of attachment, caring, and empathy. Because separation from the mother has been deemphasized, women have usually retained a strong emotional bond with their mothers in adult life.

As a result of rapid social change, adolescent girls are now asked to become like boys: to break the ties and to become independent high achievers. For young women today, the passage from adolescence to adulthood involves problems unknown to earlier generations. Society has created for them an unprecedented imperative: to alter their values and to model their adult lives not after their mothers, but after their fathers.

The women treated in the Intensive Treatment Program for Bulimia have been raised, for the most part, by mothers in traditional roles; less than 9% of the mothers of the women in the program have had jobs that required a college education (S.C. Wooley, 1985). To aspire to be a mother and homemaker is no longer enough, however. These young women must succeed on male terms, landing important jobs and demonstrating autonomy and self-reliance. Many bulimic women are angry that their mothers have not provided a life example for them to follow. They rage at the mother's "failure," while

they grieve for her restricted opportunities and sacrifices for home and family, which now command little respect.

Unable to articulate their conflicting feelings, these women are bound to their mother by a loyalty that they do not understand. Acutely sensitive to their mother's devalued position in society, the women equate the mother's problems with her body. Often, they have watched her try to diet and have observed her body hatred, for she is among the first generation of women to be exposed to society's obsession with thinness. Their own need to diet may represent their wish to escape her plight.

In this uncharted landscape, the launching of a daughter is, at best, difficult. Whether crippling psychological problems emerge depends on many factors, not all well understood. Clearly, role conflict will be heightened in proportion to the polarization in parental roles. The problem of disloyalty to the mother, embodied in rejection of her social role, will be intensified when the daughter views her mother as unhappy, lacking support from her husband, and burdened by the problems of her other children.

It appears that an important condition for bulimia exists when the daughter feels that her own most basic needs must be suppressed in the interest of the larger system. A variety of historical factors may contribute to this perception. Some women learned early in childhood that their needs would not be met or that meeting them would consume and exhaust others. Frequently, histories of bulimic women reveal unusual demands on the parents during the women's early years, such as the serious illness of a younger child, or other problems in the family. Thus, some women may have learned to be "strong" in response to parental disability, death, or divorce.

Even if the course of childhood is uneventful, the demand in adolescence to be "more like a man" may lead a woman to conceal her needs and feelings. To the extent that she equates her mother's emotional vulnerability with her apparent "failure" in modern terms and her father's emotional detachment with his worldly "success," she feels even more acutely the need to put on a false face of strength and self-assurance.

Finally, shame over needs has been found to be the residue of sexual abuse in a surprising number of patients. Half of the women treated for bulimia are victims of incest, childhood sexual molestation, or rape (Wooley & Kearney-Cooke, 1986). Like most victims of abuse, they blame themselves: "If I hadn't been so needy, if I hadn't needed my father's [uncle's, neighbor's] affection, this would not have happened to me." This shame not only suppresses the experience and expression of needs, but also increases body hatred. Relief of shame will be found, the bulimic hopes, in self-purification by the avoidance of food, physical conditioning, and the almost literal demolition of the body.

The alternation of eating and purging constitutes a perfect metaphor for the emotional neediness and repudiation of needs that underlie the symptoms. The task of treatment is to redirect the expression of these conflicting impulses from the physical to the emotional realm, bringing the needs into the open where they can be understood, validated, and met.

PROGRAM FORMAT

The Intensive Treatment Program for Bulimia consists of six closely integrated components:

1. a daily food group. Using daily food records, the food group begins the task of teaching patients the practical changes that they must make to overcome bulimia, especially the establishment of regular meals and regular meal times and the inclusion of previously "forbidden foods." It also examines the ways in which weight and eating are used as communications both inside and outside the family, and the ways in which they are symptoms of tensions around the definition of one's own and others' needs. Detailed discussion of the physiology of bulimia and the process of recovery can be found in earlier papers (Wooley & Wooley, 1985; Wooley & Kearney-Cooke, 1986).

2. a daily psychotherapy group. The psychotherapy group uses dialogue and role play to illuminate family issues and to prepare patients to address in the multifamily meeting the concerns that they have identified as crucial. After the multi-family meeting, the group is used to identify and change the ways that the women perpetuate their family roles with peers. In addition, the barriers to intimacy that have grown out of family loyalties are challenged.

3. daily body image therapy. The body image group uses the woman's experience of her body—the terms in which she has cast her problems—to understand issues in the mother-

daughter bond, the changes within the family triggered by the daughter's puberty, parental and sibling rivalry and competition, and the development of sexuality. Because of the inherent limitations of words, these themes are explored through imagery, art, and movement. While the particular content of the group therapy is often inappropriate for family discussion, the issues that emerge are often family ones.

4. two or three individual sessions per week. Individual therapy is used to help the patient conceptualize and integrate what she is learning in each modality and to experience an intimate relationship with a nonparental adult.

5. two or three educational seminars per week. Educational seminars focus not only on the physiological bases of weight regulation and eating disorders, but also on the symbolic cultural meanings of thinness and feminist analyses of dieting.

6. family therapy, consisting primarily of a 2-day multifamily session.

There is a consistent staff for all six components, and they meet daily to exchange information. The various forms of therapy are considered different techniques to explore the same issues as they are expressed in different ways.

FAMILY THERAPY COMPONENT

The 2-day multi-family group therapy sessions are held 10 days after the program begins. Each woman invites her family of origin, including divorced parents; her immediate family, including ents; her immediate family, including her children who are over 7 years old, and, as seems appropriate, her in-laws; and key members of the extended family. Since family members come from all over the country, the 2-day meeting is feasible in terms of time, money, and energy. Furthermore, it parallels the intensity of the program itself.

Multi-family groups, first devised by Laqueur (Laqueur, LaBurt, & Morong, 1964), have grown to be a powerful, effective treatment modality (Gritzer & Okun, 1983; Strelnick, 1977). They offer the advantages of family therapy—an opportunity to see the family together, to assess the dysfunctional patterns, and to suggest means for change—as well as the advantages of group therapy—mutual support and confrontation. In the program, both aspects of the multi-family groups are used. At times, the boundaries around each family are emphasized; at other times, the family lines are diffused while the family roles—mother, father, sibling, husband, child—are stressed.

Family members and patients stay in the same hotel. The sessions take place in a room that is large enough to move around in, yet small enough to reinforce the message that "we are all in this together." At each session, there are 30 to 45 patients and family members, who are usually from at least three generations, and six staff members, who meet periodically throughout each day to share information and discuss strategies.

For the sake of clarity, the multi-family group treatment can be described in three distinct stages: education, assessment, and change. In actual practice, however, there is no such precise distinction.

Education

Family members often come to the sessions with little or no accurate information about bulimia. Thus, the therapists open the multi-family group sessions with a short lecture addressed to the questions: How does bulimia begin? What maintains it? What must happen to produce a cure? This introduces in the least threatening way some of the issues likely to be addressed in the following 2 days: the bulimic woman's habitual concealment of her real feelings; the role of bulimia in avoiding separation and masking family problems; and the high incidence of sexual abuse among bulimics. Families are also told what to expect during the recovery process: all symptoms may not disappear immediately, the return to normal eating may mean an initial weight gain, and the woman may be more assertive. The lecture format gives the families time to adapt to their surroundings before any demands are made of them.

Assessment

During the second stage of the multi-family group, therapists assess family relationships: the triangles, the distorted perceptions that the women have of their family, the sequential behavior patterns, the family myths, and the family's flexibility and ability to change. The assessment begins by having each family construct a genogram. Sitting in their own family circle on the floor, family members are given a large sheet of paper and markers, and later a list of personality styles and behaviors that are relevant to bulimia. The traits on this list can be varied, but they usually include controlling behavior, anger, conflict avoidance, difficulty separating, problems with drugs and alcohol, perfectionism, sexual issues (including abuse), body image problems, physical and mental health problems. Then each family is asked to color-code its genogram. Thus, for example, everyone in the family who is a perfectionist is circled in blue; everyone who has difficulty with separation, in purple. The colors help the families see patterns.

Therapists make no interpretations; they only ask the family what patterns they see and what they can learn from the color-coded genograms. The major goals of this task are to help the families look into transgenerational family relationships, to give therapists information about the family across several generations, and to allow therapists to observe the families as they interact around an assigned task. The process by which they perform the task is often as important as the content.

Often, family members take this opportunity to share secret information. In one family, the 17-year old brother drew a line for an out-of-wedlock son previously unknown to the others. In another family, the bulimic woman discovered her natural father's name, which her mother had always refused to tell her.

Having just been unified by the joint task, the families are then separated into role groups. Mothers, fathers, husbands, siblings, and children meet those in their same role in other families and discuss their feelings about their particular relationship to a bulimic woman. This helps loosen the familial glue and develop support across family boundaries. Throughout the 2 days, role groups are occasionally reassembled to give support or problem-solving assistance to one another.

To start the therapeutic process, the therapist works with one spotlighted family. This family sits in a circle in the middle of the room. Members of other families sit behind their role counterpart (e.g., mothers sit behind the mother, siblings behind the siblings). They are all told that, while members of the spotlighted family will be talking about their own family's issues, their feelings are probably similar to those of many others in the group. Anyone is free to speak to the spotlighted family member in the same role or to speak for that person to another spotlighted family member.

Dramatic moments engage the group, and the shared relief establishes the value of airing private business in the group. The mutuality of the experience defuses the fear of exposure in front of others. Some participants take this opportunity to talk to members of their own family through the spotlighted family. Approached in this way, confrontation or exposure of fears may be easier. On some issues, the role groups divide by sexes. For example, the women may confront the men over their detachment from the family and their overinvolvement in work. Sometimes, specific themes cut across families.

Joyce, a 27-year-old married woman, told her mother that she had felt abandoned by her. Her mother had devoted her time to her own aged mother, who had lived with them since Joyce was a child. She was represented in the room by an empty chair containing her apron and placed between Joyce and her mother. While Joyce talked, her mother sat impassively. When the therapist asked her if she had felt torn between her daughter and her mother, she began to cry. She knew that her mother had needed her, while Joyce had been such a responsible and self-reliant oldest child. When the therapist asked her to change seats with "Grandma," she immediately leaned over and hugged her daughter. They both wept, as did the other family members. It was as if the grandmother's seat had forcibly kept them apart.

The therapist asked if there was another mother in the room who understood what Joyce's mother was feeling. Mrs. P., who had until this moment put forth the image of a perfect mother in a perfect family, started to cry. She wondered if her daughter Patty felt the same way, because during Patty's early years Mr. and Mrs. P. had directed much of their attention to a retarded daughter who was 1 year older than Patty. Several mothers leaned over and put an arm around Mrs. P. as she wept.

Change

Having identified some of the dysfunctional behavioral interactions of the families, therapists then create situations within the room to block or alter their typical patterns. Exercises created during this stage focus on dyadic, triadic, and full family relationships. The themes grow out of issues raised during the 2 days of multi-family therapy or during the first week of the treatment program. Some of the more common issues are

- problems in separation
- the inability to express anger within the family

- perception of the mother as fragile or ineffectual

- perceived emotional distance of the father

- unexpressed sexual tension between the father and the bulimic daughter

- siblings' extreme symmetrical or complementary relationships

- parental disagreement in dealing with the "sick" daughter

- bulimia as a form of "loyalty" to one or several family members

- the homeostatic role that bulimia plays in the family

Exercises developed to explore and rework these issues vary with each group and must be responsive to the group's particular needs.

One exercise was spontaneously devised to deal with separation when bulimic twin sisters talked about the difficulty of leaving one another and their mother. This paralleled the separation issue that other families were discussing. Therefore, a birthing exercise was created, whereby mothers and fathers reexperienced through role play the anticipatory pregnancy period—the closeness, separateness, fears, and hopes that each had had. Then, using long pieces of material to represent the birth canal, each mother held one end while her bulimic daughter, as the child in utero, held the other. As a representation of labor, each mother slowly moved around the room, pulling on her end of the material. The "baby" passively held on. As a metaphor for the actual birth, each was told to let go of her end of the material at a specified moment. The emotional responses to the "letting go"

powerfully reflected the current ambivalent feelings about separation.

An exercise developed to mobilize anger and identify disparate factions within the family is the "protectors and fed-uppers." The bulimic women are asked to line up in the middle of the room. Members of each family decide if they feel more protective of the bulimic or more "fed up" with her and her illness. The protectors in each family stand in front of the bulimic woman, guarding her. The "fed-uppers" are instructed to capture her, take her to their side of the room, and tell her why they are fed up—often for the first time—without any intervention from the protector. The protectors gather in a group to discuss what it means to leave the bulimic woman alone with the fed-uppers. They are often fearful for the bulimic woman, as well as for themselves; they have no control over what is happening, and they are, essentially, jobless.

The common problems of unexpressed anger between mother and daughter, and each one's fear of weakness in the other have been addressed in pushing matches. With hands pressed against each other, each mother-daughter pair makes angry noises and pushes the other as hard as possible. In order to demonstrate systemic involvement metaphorically, the therapists ask each father to make sure that neither woman gets hurt and to support his wife physically if she needs extra power. The siblings' task is to critique the efforts of mother, sister, and father. The metaphors for the family roles are never delineated, but the messages are heard. Typical comments afterward include "I feel proud I didn't give in; I always do." "I'm surprised; I thought I would hurt her, but she is stronger than I thought.'' Some fathers find it difficult to support their wives, feeling drawn to their daughters. Others are surprised and relieved to see that each woman can protect herself. Siblings often identify avoidance of the task by their mother, sister or father, saying ''It is just like it is at home.''

Separate exercises are often devised for specific dyads (e.g., fathers and bulimic daughters, bulimic wives and husbands) or for subgroups (e.g., siblings). Fathers and daughters may be asked to tell each other one or two things that they need from the other, for example. Problems in sibling relationships receive special attention. Siblings need to express their anger at being overlooked by their parents or shut out by their bulimic sister; they are needed to pull the bulimic sister from her entanglement with the parents. Exercises specific to bulimic women and their husbands often come at the end of the multi-family group sessions, reflecting the developmental life cycle. Husbands are crucial peers who can free the bulimic women from their family-of-origin enmeshment.

In preparation for change, families may be asked to use their bodies to make a ''live'' sculpture illustrating their power or dependency relationships (Duhl, Kantor, & Duhl, 1973). When a consensus has been reached, members are asked to reflect on the ways in which the status quo suits their personal needs. Once the benefits of the status quo have been acknowledged, they are asked to consider changes that they would like and to create a new sculpture.

The multi-family sessions always end with the parents seated separately from their children, demonstrating the need for generational divisions. In the ''hello-goodbye'' exercise, each family is lined up separately, and the bulimic woman divides the members into two groups: those with whom she needs more emotional distance and those with whom she needs more closeness. She is then asked to explain to each person in the first group why she needs to move on and to say goodbye; this is often a tearful exchange. She then turns to those in the second group and, in effect, says hello, explaining what she needs from them and why she needs them in her life. Those from the goodbye line, composed primarily of parents, gather in a group to discuss what the separation will mean for them.

The hello-goodbye exercise elicits recurrent issues. The bulimic daughter wonders if her parents can make it on their own; she wonders if she herself can. Siblings talk of the space that they can now enter with parents, space that has been filled by the bulimic sister, and of the potential for a better sibling relationship. Parents talk about their differences in dealing with their bulimic daughter, their own marital problems, and the need to rearrange their lives. A common response of husbands was summed up by one who said, at the end of the exercise, ''Jane and I were married 6 months ago, but we really were married these past 2 days. I want to thank all you people for being a part of our wedding.''

INTEGRATION OF FAMILY ISSUES WITH OTHER PROGRAM COMPONENTS

Obviously, not all problems can be resolved in 2 days. Each family identifies the key issues in the 2 days, however, and the bulimic woman has the rest of the program to work on them. The benefit of family therapy lies not only in its power to resolve family problems, but also in its power to expose the template that the individual applies to all other interpersonal experience. Family life forever influences the ways in which family members understand and respond to the actions of others.

As family issues are duplicated in transferences to group members and to therapists, references to the shared experiences of the multi-family session may help the women understand their problems in relating to one another. The task for the therapists is to help integrate the information learned and the changes begun during the multi-family group sessions with the rest of the therapies and to keep identifying the disabling transferences.

In the first week of the program, Carol's haughty demeanor gave way to the tremendous neediness she felt. The oldest and most successful in the group, she was nonetheless jealous of the attention that the others received and charged the group with holding her success against her and excluding her. She saw this as a continuation of a family pattern in which, as the oldest, she had received little mothering and was shut out by her siblings, who were envious of her status.

As these issues were aired in the multi-family group, Carol learned that her sisters avoided her because they felt that she looked down on them. She never went to their houses and, on family occasions, directed her attention to her father. While admitting that he liked his discussions with her, her father urged her to rejoin her siblings. Her mother acknowledged that Carol had never been allowed to be a child and then tearfully rocked her in her lap.

After the multi-family sessions, Carol felt better; however, she continued to discount the suggestions and invitations of her "siblings" in the group, turning instead to the therapists. One day, criticized by Carol for not being sensitive to her, another patient shouted, "But you don't take anything we try to give!" Again and again, Carol was reminded of the ways in which she reenacted her old family situation until, at last, she began to find even improbable opportunities to get closer to the others, such as sleeping over in their rooms. The change was apparent in the softening of her face and a new infectious laugh.

Maura had won early sympathy from the group by describing her parents' absence the weekend that she was crowned Homecoming Queen and revealing her loneliness and vulnerability. She still missed her father, who had divorced her mother when Maura was a young child, and she described her stepfather as critical and overbearing. Her frequent binges were accompanied by panic attacks.

Maura's mother, father, stepfather, and sister came to the multi-family session. She told her father how much his failure to call had hurt her. Awkward, he explained that he had stayed away in deference to her stepfather. This had perhaps been unfortunate for her stepfather who, although clearly an aggressive man, was also a warm one. He confronted Maura on her 12-year pattern of rejecting him. "I can understand that you are reluctant to get close to another father," he explained, "but even if your mother and I were to divorce, I would always love and want to see you." Although her mother wept, Maura remained unresponsive.

During the next week of the program, Maura was pleasant and cheerful to everyone, but close to none. Her binges continued, and she never sought help at the time she felt the urge to binge. The other women began to point out that Maura was excluding them, just as she excluded her stepfather. In a re-creation of the night that her natural father had left, she was able to experience closeness with a role-played sibling. In an exercise in which she was allowed to control the physical distance between herself and others, she overcame a recurrent feeling of panic that she related to her stepfather's tendency to be physically intrusive, an experience validated by others who had found his hugs somewhat uncomfortable. At last, she was truly able to admit peers into her inner life when, in following a therapist's suggestion to share the frenzy of a binge with someone, she found the frenzy replaced by an experience of intimacy that virtually transformed her. After the program, the therapists learned that Maura had stopped bingeing, found it easy to talk to both

her mother and stepfather, and was much closer to friends.

Greta had been bulimic as well as overweight for many years and was a veteran of many therapies, most of which had ended because of boundary violations. She presented an almost overwhelming array of physical and psychological problems, including allergies; migraines; edema; sexual, marital, and vocational difficulties; and a history of sexual molestation by a brother and a previous therapist.

Although she was totally unable to articulate what she needed to say to her parents in the multi-family group, she did grasp that it was important for her to dress like an attractive, grown woman. When she told her rather distant and defensive mother of the pain she had felt because, as a fat child, she had not been able to go to her mother for support, her mother responded with nurturance. Greta used the rest of the session to work on separating from her parents and becoming closer to her husband. An unfinished problem was her projection onto her husband of a hatred of her body.

In a body image session shortly after the multi-family sessions, the therapist asked the women to be their mothers at a small "tea party." After they had walked about, playing their roles, the therapist asked them to line up according to who was the prettiest. The week before, when they had done this for themselves, Greta had placed herself last. This time, in the role of her mother, Greta fought to be first, pushing out two other determined contenders and winning.

In the discussion that followed, the others expressed surprise at Greta's behavior. They had not considered Greta's mother so attractive that she should have first place. Greta then told the group that her mother had been a stunning young woman and had given up a career in the theater to raise a family. Greta let go of a family myth when she then acknowledged that her mother had become an old-looking alcoholic. As she continued talking, she came to an important realization: her mother's dissatisfaction with her may not have been due to her fat body, but due to her mother's resentment over her own lost prospects. Greta began to laugh uncontrollably—partly out of relief, partly out of sadness for what she and her mother had lost.

Later that week, she dressed up as the "blob" she had imagined herself to be, having so much fun that the impact of the costume was nearly lost. In a dialogue with her mother, she said that she was moving on to her own life. She allowed a greater closeness with the others. Two weeks after the program ended, she walked confidently in a bathing suit on a Florida beach and reported that her physical symptoms had all disappeared.

Paula was a 19-year-old college sophomore, bulimic for 4 years and getting steadily worse. Lively and engaging, but uncomfortable in her generous body, she seemed like an animated rag mop. Failing her classes, retreating from friends, and

trying unsuccessfully to hold two jobs, she at last withdrew from school to enter the Intensive Treatment Program. The youngest in the group, she fought to be everyone's care-giver, expressing her own problems only through uncontrolled eating and occasional outbursts of confused frustration.

When Paula was 8, her father left her mother for her mother's best friend. Paula remained with her mother until her sophomore year in high school, when she went to live with her father and stepmother. She had worked with a previous therapist on the impact of her depressed mother's neglect of her and Paula's caretaking of her mother after the divorce.

In the multi-family session, tensions among the adults in Paula's family erupted almost immediately, when Claire, the stepmother, used the genogram to refer to a secret abortion that Mary, the mother, had undergone during her marriage to Mike, the father. Within the 2 days, however, the adults began taking better care of themselves and one another. Claire supported Mary in an effort to set limits on Paula. With coaching, Mike was able to join his wife in taking a firmer stand with Paula. The two mothers united in their efforts to keep Paula's grandmother from undermining their discipline. In a 4-hour discussion that night, they made up their differences over the years and continued, after the multi-family group sessions, to cooperate closely on plans for Paula. Paula expressed delight and cried with relief, however, she bolted down several beers during a break.

After the multi-family sessions, Paula struggled with her ambivalence about remaining in a caretaker-caregiver relationship versus becoming independent, symbolized for her by her body size. In body image therapy, it was discovered that her voluptuous body carried important meanings for her; it attracted men who, if she took care of them, in turn cared for her. This association went back to sexual molestation at puberty by a loving uncle. The thinness to which she aspired represented a somewhat frightening level of independence. Not surprisingly, Paula had found it easier to give up purging than to give up bingeing and overeating.

In an enactment of separation in a therapy group, she was tugged by parents and peers. Practicing an imaginary telephone call to her father a year later, she found it difficult to give up his care and to deprive him of his job of worrying about her. One of the few times that she cried in individual therapy was when she realized how much she worried about her father, who had gone bankrupt and was not working.

In the final week, there were important indications of Paula's emerging self-differentiation and separation. She realized that she had been waiting for her roommate to succeed before she herself succeeded. She refused to help her roommate when it conflicted with her own needs. She made appropriate requests of the group for help. She decided not to return to either family after the program, but to return to school. She became accepting not only of her weight and her needs, but also of the responsibility for finding appropriate ways to meet her needs.

CONCLUSION

There seems little doubt that the multi-family group sessions open channels of communication and offer new options for relationships inside the family and new hope for relationships outside of it. The multi-family group therapy is only a beginning, however; there is much more to recovery from bulimia than improved family relationships. These women must change their eating patterns, make peace with their body, and learn to establish and maintain peer relationships. Furthermore, many of the women have intrapsychic issues that persist beyond the cure of bulimia.

The modification of eating requires a neutral, supportive coach with technical expertise. Improved peer relations require practice so that interaction patterns learned within the family can be identified and changed. Body image disturbance must be explored in privacy and reworked with the use of specialized, often nonverbal, techniques. Further, the patient will require a relationship with a supportive adult who, unlike family members, does not require care-taking. Then she can have an optimal opportunity to explore and express her own feelings.

When the program ends, recommendations are made for continuing work. In some instances, these recommendations include additional family therapy or, for local patients, participation in a weekly multi-family group. In many cases, however, the major follow-up is individual and/or group therapy by the patient's referring therapist in her home town.

Early results from 1-year follow-up show an average reduction in binge-purge frequency of 91% (Wooley & Kearney-Cooke, 1986). In addition, significant and substantial improvements on all measures of psychological function achieved during the program show no tendency to regress in the following year, but instead show continuing improvement. These measures include the Eating Attitudes Test, Eating Disorders Inventory, Restraint Scale, Self-Cathexis Scale, Body Cathexis Scale, Color-a-Person Test, and Hopkins SCL-90 (see Wooley & Kearney-Cooke, 1986).

These results demonstrate the substantial gains which can be made when family interventions are integrated into a comprehensive program addressing the problem of bulimia from multiple vantage points. Even patients with severe and longstanding bulimia and significant accompanying psychopathology can usually be substantially helped.

REFERENCES

Chodorow, N. (1978). *The reproduction of mothering*. Berkeley and Los Angeles: University of California Press.

Duhl, F., Kantor, D., and Duhl, B. (1973). Learning, space, and action in family therapy: A primer in sculpture. In D.A. Bloch (Ed.), *Techniques of family psychotherapy: A primer*. New York: Grune & Stratton.

Gilligan, C. (1982). *In a different voice*. Cambridge, MA: Harvard University Press.

Gritzer, P.H., & Okun, H.S. (1983). Multiple family group therapy: A model for all families. In B.B. Wolman & G. Stricker (Eds.), *Handbook of family and marital therapy*. New York: Plenum Press.

Laqueur, H.P., LaBurt, H.A., & Morong, E. (1964). Multiple family therapy. In J.H. Masserman (Ed.), *Current psychiatric therapies* (Vol. 4). New York: Grune & Stratton.

Strelnick, A.H. (1977). Multiple family group therapy: A review of the literature. *Family Process, 16,* 307–325.

Wooley, S.C. (August 1985). Role conflict, body image, and eating disorders. Paper presentation at the American Psychological Association.

Wooley, S.C., & Kearney-Cooke, A. (1986). Intensive treatment of bulimia and body image disturbance. In K. Brownell & J. Foreyt (Eds.), *Physiology, psychology and the treatment of eating disorders*. New York: Basic Books.

Wooley, S.C., & Wooley, O.W. (1985). Intensive residential and outpatient treatment of bulimia. In D. Garner & P. Garfinkel (Eds.), *Handbook of psychotherapy for anorexia nervosa and bulimia* (pp. 391–430). New York: Guilford Press.

3

Couple Therapy for Bulimia

Mary Jo Barrett
Director
Midwest Family Resource
Chicago, Illinois
  and
Richard Schwartz
Co-ordinator of Training and Research
Institute for Juvenile Research
Chicago, Illinois

BULIMIA, BINGEING ON FOOD and subsequent purging, is a dangerous behavior that is practiced by women in epidemic numbers (Boskind-White & White, 1983). Most of the literature and subsequent treatment of bulimia focuses on the individual (Bruch, 1973, 1978; Casper, 1983; Garner & Garfinkel, 1985) and her family of origin (Schwartz, 1986; Schwartz, Barrett, & Saba, 1985). Little attention has been paid to the couple relationship as a meaningful context that maintains the symptom of bulimia.

ASSESSMENT

The bulimic marries, cohabitates with or becomes involved in a primary relationship with a person who makes it possible for her to continue her relationship with food and, therefore, with bulimia.* In a complementary manner, the relationship that she chooses also helps her to remain involved in the dysfunctional patterns of her own and her spouse's family of origin. Thus, it is useful to have information about the family backgrounds, developmental stage of the couple, the chronicity of the symptom, the presence of other symptoms, and other pertinent life situations, when making an assessment.

The five patterns that Minuchin, Rosman, and Baker (1978) found in psychosomatic families can be found in the families of bulimics as well; three more patterns are specific to bulimia:

1. enmeshment and disengagement. The family tends to oscillate between

---

*The majority of clients have been women, therefore the use of the feminine pronoun.

extreme involvement and almost total abandonment.

2. overprotectiveness. The woman's family of origin and her spouse tend to be overprotective, keeping the woman from growing up and facing the conflicts of adult life.

3. rigidity. Interactions and reactions in the family are repetitive. Family members respond to one another with a set of emotional sequences that seldom allow individuation, flexibility, or independent alternatives.

4. lack of conflict resolution. Conflicts in the family, individuals, and marriages do not end. Individual members do not learn the skills required to resolve conflicts and, thus, become fearful of potential problem areas in their lives.

5. overinvolvement in the parental subsystem. The bulimic, whether living with her parents or not, is usually very involved in their relationship. She may spend an inordinate amount of time worrying about their relationship or discussing their relationship with one or both of them.

6. isolation. Members of a bulimic's family are likely to rely solely on each other to meet their emotional needs, believing that they should not need anyone outside their family. Without feedback from extrafamilial sources, however, families can become stagnant and even more rigid in their dysfunctional patterns.

7. overemphasis on appearance. The family overemphasizes physical and social appearances, both those within the family and those in relation to others. They do not seek the feedback of others; they simply want to look good at all times.

8. special meaning to food and eating. The family uses food and eating experiences as avenues of communication. They show love by dispensing food and displeasure by withdrawing it. Family occasions are frequently punctuated by a meal, and many negative interactions take place when they gather to eat. As a result, the significance of food goes beyond physical sustenance.

Because these patterns of behavior have become an integral part of the bulimic's relationships, they can also be found in the bulimic's marital system. The interactional sequences may function to maintain the symptom, but conversely the symptom may function to maintain the interaction of the couple. For example, a couple may remain enmeshed through their concern about the bulimia, or they may avoid conflict by always focusing on the binge-purge sequence.

Bulimia has six predominant functions for a couple; it

1. allows the woman to remain involved with her family while also being involved with her spouse

2. allows continued avoidance of conflict and lack of conflict resolution, both within the woman herself and in her relationships

3. maintains a structure of extreme complementarity within the couple

4. distracts the couple from other problems

5. helps regulate the balance of power and control in the marital system

6. regulates proximity and distance

It can be assumed that two individuals are attracted to one another based on each individual's expectation that the other can fulfill his or her needs. Obviously, these needs are derived from their experiences in their family of origin. The coupling is successful if the two persons involved remain flexible in the face of their potentially conflicting set of needs. In the case of a couple involved in bulimia, the bulimic person has generally been engaged in bulimic behaviors before she meets her mate. She chooses someone who permits and needs the bulimia and the associated behaviors (e.g., dependency, lack of intimacy). Their individual and couple needs are met through a physically and emotionally dangerous symptom that does not allow the flexibility necessary for growth.

Connection to Family of Origin

The relationship between the bulimic and her spouse mirrors the marital relationship of the bulimic's parents. The dysfunctional patterns of interactions in her family of origin, such as lack of conflict resolution and inappropriate boundaries between parent and child, are duplicated in her marriage. At the same time, her interaction with her spouse mirrors her interactions with her parents. In other words, she fluctuates between being spouse and being child to her mate, while her mate fluctuates between being spouse and being parent to her.

Not only do the couple's interactions replicate the interactional patterns of the bulimic's family, but also the nature of the couple's interaction allows the woman to continue her dysfunctional interactions with her family. She remains their bulimic daughter, for whom they

feel either total dedication or repulsion. Usually, the parents oscillate between these two extreme positions. In any case, they are intensely involved with their daughter's emotional life. The woman's bulimia guarantees her loyalty to her family through her involvement with them, as well as through her dysfunctional interactions with her spouse.

Internal Conflicts

The conflicts that were unresolved in the woman's family of origin continue to be unresolved in her adult married life (Schwartz et al., 1985). She is confused by the rules that her family and society have constructed with respect to her role as a woman. It is impossible for a woman to fulfill perfectly and simultaneously the roles of person, spouse, mother, and child. Yet, many women try to do so, expecting perfection from themselves.

Failure to meet these impossible demands presents a woman with a burdensome conflict. The binge-purge episodes can physically and emotionally nullify her thoughts and feelings. Temporarily, she resolves the conflict and avoids the burdensome feelings by ridding herself of what is inside her. The bulimia protects her from the demands of society, spouse, and self—and, consequently, all the conflicts associated with these contexts. She is anesthetized, which helps her cope with her life as a woman. Clearly, the bulimia is an illusionary solution to her internal conflicts and a metaphorical attempt to have and do it all.

Complementarity of the Couple

Paradoxically, the binge-purge sequence helps a person avoid role definition as an individual, yet defines the roles of both spouses in the marriage. Placing a couple in a category is a subjective process that can be helpful in establishing a baseline of behaviors, but it must be remembered that all couples are unique, even in the way that they are similar.

Over-Responsible/Under-Responsible

In a rigidly stable form of complementarity, the over-responsible/under-responsible couple has many of the characteristics of alcoholic couples (Bepko & Krestan, 1985). Like the nondrinker, the nonbulimic is dedicated to being competent and helpful. His purpose is to keep his life in order so that he can save his spouse from the bulimia. When the bulimic exhibits out-of-control behaviors that leave her physically and emotionally drained, incompetent, and dependent, the nonbingeing partner assumes an over-responsible posture, the behavior of both partners is thus extreme. In the context of the relationship, the over-responsible mate is seen as tolerant, sacrificing, and good. The bulimic's under-responsible behavior allows him to maintain the image of himself as strong and competent.

The under-responsible partner is at the same time in a powerful and powerless position. Her power comes from the fact that the world revolves around her. Her spouse attempts to meet her needs and protect her, treating her as a child. She is powerless, however, when her weak position allows others to take control.

The surrender of these positions constitutes a major shift in the lives of both parties and involves dramatic risks. The incompetent, under-responsible bulimic would have to give up attention, help, and protection; she would have to assume more responsibility in her mar-

riage, her family, and her larger context. The spouse, in the one-up position, is insulated by his wall of goodness and strength. Without his partner's bulimia, he would have to take more responsibility for himself and less for others. The bulimia provides a comfortable balance for the couple.

Mutually Over-Responsible/Under-Responsible

Each member of the mutually over-responsible/under-responsible couple oscillates between under- and over-responsible postures. They each play both the parent and the child roles at different times. The positions are determined by their respective symptoms at a given time. For example, the nonbulimic spouse may become alcoholic, chronically depressed, or suicidal; he may experience severe financial or employment problems. With the appearance of his symptom, he becomes the incompetent, and the bulimic spouse becomes the care-giver. At some point, the bulimic then becomes overwhelmed and withdraws through the bulimia. As the relationship then has no responsible "executive," the nonbulimic spouse responds by assuming the responsible position. This constant shift provides the couple with periods of both intense closeness and prolonged withdrawal. At times, it appears that they may have the best of both worlds: both parent and child. The chaos that ensues is exhausting and rarely rewarding, however.

The rigid imbalanced nature of the relationship of the mutually over-responsible/under-responsible couple becomes cemented by the repetition of the bulimia. With each binge-purge sequence, they become more and more deeply entrenched in their complementary positions.

Distraction

Bulimia can distract a couple from other problems, such as those associated with family relationships, financial matters, or children. A couple can easily focus on the "sick" spouse as the source of the family problems instead of challenging the "well" family members to examine their own roles and difficulties. The distraction is particularly important for a couple who need to avoid conflict. The bulimia can become an integral part of their relationship; the longer the bulimia protects them from the struggles of married life, the more necessary it becomes.

Regulation of Power and Control

When a woman experiences a loss of control and a sense of powerlessness in a relationship, bulimia may help her to gain a more powerful position. The bulimia is a behavior that no one else can control. It is also a method of communication. Through the bingeing and purging, the woman voices her displeasure with the world, the family, the marriage, and herself. This may be the only way that she asserts herself and lets her feelings and opinions be known, albeit indirectly. Thus, not only does she temporarily release her internal pressures through bingeing and purging, but also she communicates her dissatisfactions, leaving her a bit more uncontrollably in control.

Bulimia may also be an attempt to regain lost power. The bulimic experiences her power through her spouse's profuse exclamations of his powerlessness. Once again, it is not a very direct or satisfying experience of power. Angry

about the incompetent child role she plays in the marriage, a part of her desires more power. Another part of her is afraid of assuming power, however. The bulimia appears to be the perfect solution to the power problem. The woman can gain power indirectly without overtly unbalancing the marital power structure.

Regulation of Proximity and Distance

Closeness and distance are frequently governed by the binge-purge sequence. Many times, the bulimia is the catalyst that allows the couple to regain closeness after a period of distance. Responding to the bulimia often takes priority over any other situation, and the couple join forces to meet the villain. They often dare to discuss sensitive topics or engage in sexual intimacy. The intimacy seems less risky to them, because they are attempting to understand the "whys" of the bulimia and to comfort one another. These moments of intimacy are homeostatic. As they begin to move closer to one another and communicate more directly, they are protected from too much closeness by the woman's distraught behavior and by the man's focus on her as the problem. When the conversation or the sexual proximity becomes too intimate or too frustrating, either party can withdraw. Subsequently, either partner can retrieve the proximity by asking for or offering help.

Although the intimacy that the woman has with the bulimia creates distance in the marriage, it also protects the couple from infidelity. The woman is as intimately involved with the ritual of bingeing and purging as she might be with a lover; it provides for her what the marriage does not. The nonbingeing spouse tends to remain faithful because of his overinvolvement in his wife's symptom. The bulimia and the related symptoms of both spouses become a third party in the marriage; there is no need for a third person.

STAGES AND TECHNIQUES OF COUPLE THERAPY

When treating bulimia, the therapist must change the dysfunctional interactional patterns that maintain the bulimic behaviors. These sequences do not originate or exist solely within the couple, but the couple system is currently most involved. Therefore, the treatment model begins with marital therapy and addresses this unit throughout therapy. Individual and extended family sessions are held concurrently, depending on the nature of the case.

The basic concepts for this treatment model are influenced by the structural (Minuchin, 1974; Minuchin & Fishman, 1981; Minuchin et al., 1978) and the strategic (Fisch, Weakland, & Segal, 1982; Haley, 1976; Madanes, 1981; Selvini-Palazzoli, Boscolo, Cecchin, & Prata, 1978) schools of family therapy. Interventions are aimed at restructuring the couple's interactions so that they no longer continue dysfunctional patterns and family structures. The goals of treatment are to help the man and woman, individually and as a unit, create a context that can support

1. a vast reduction in bulimic behavior. Total abstinence is optimal, but many clients consider treatment that results in no more than periodic binges a success.

2. interactional sequences that are flexible and independent of the bulimic behavior.

3. comfortable boundaries, as defined by the couple, between them and their families.

4. interdependent functioning by both partners.

5. a change in the couple's self-perception individually and as a unit.

The clinician observes and tracks the interactions that maintain the symptom, explores with the dyad the functions that the bulimia serves in their marriage and with their families, and intervenes with both in-session and between-session tasks. Integrating the structural and strategic models of therapy necessitates both directly challenging the couple and restraining them from change. The rhythm is a response to the couple's ambivalence regarding change and a reflection of the belief that resistance to change is natural. Based on this belief system and this style of therapeutic intervention, the treatment model is divided into three flexible stages: (1) creating a context for change, (2) challenging patterns and expanding alternatives, and (3) consolidating changes. These stages provide a general therapeutic framework that can be adapted to the idiosyncratic nature of each case.

Stage 1: Creating a Context for Change

The couple and their families have created and lived in an environment that is highly conducive to symptomatic behavior. The therapist must help the couple begin to create a context that does not maintain rigid dysfunctional patterns.

The first stage is a definition stage; the therapist and clients find a common language to define the problem, shifting the emphasis from the bulimia and placing it on dysfunctional patterns. The new context is created and the problem defined by establishing a relationship between couple and therapist, gathering information and then creating therapeutic realities, acknowledging the negative consequences of change, and restraining the change.

Establishing a Relationship

The therapist must establish himself or herself as the expert from the beginning of the treatment. Those who suffer from anorexia nervosa and/or bulimia tend to be self-made experts on the subject of their condition, and it is imperative that therapists avoid engaging in a power struggle with the client. When this happens, the therapist must reestablish leadership by making his or her conceptualization of the problem and model of therapy absolutely clear to the couple.

After the therapist is established as a trusting and caring expert, the next step is to determine a medical baseline for the bulimic. Bulimia is a physiologically impairing disorder that must be monitored and treated medically. A physician is involved in the case from the beginning and should be consulted regularly throughout the course of treatment, depending on the condition of the client.

During the first session, it is helpful to give a brief lecture on bulimia in order to

1. help establish the therapist as the expert and communicate therapeutic biases
2. begin to build the themes for the therapy

3. challenge some of the couple's realities in a less threatening manner

With this intervention the therapist creates a positive frame. In order to normalize the problem, the therapist tries to share a few general concepts, letting the couple know that he or she understands their problems and tries planting seeds for the themes that he or she is planning to use in treatment. For this reason, the therapist may mention such topics as conflict resolution, family of origin, and mutual protection. Abuse is mentioned in the first session because a large percentage of bulimics have in fact been abused, particularly sexually (Schwartz, Barret, & Saba, in press). The client who has been abused thus learns that the therapist is prepared to discuss such abuse and that it will have to be disclosed eventually. Finally, the therapist suggests that the couple begin to think of the ways that the bulimia is helpful to them.

Gathering Information and Creating Therapeutic Realities

Stage 1 establishes the themes that are used throughout therapy. The first several sessions provide opportunities to build general themes that may be expanded throughout treatment. The therapist gathers the information to build these themes through questions that make it possible to track the couple's interactions and through enactments that illustrate interactional patterns. The therapist asks questions about the symptomatic behavior, the couple's responses to it, and their hypothesis of how and why the symptom occurs. Further questioning explores the involvement of both extended families in the attempted solutions to the problem. In order to identify the couple's interactional patterns, the therapist may ask them to discuss with one another in session a current problem, the role of their families in their lives, or other unresolved conflicts. The content of such an enactment is not as important as the process and style of their communication.

The therapist may also assign the bulimic the task of keeping a journal of the bulimic episodes in order to gather data. The client logs in the journal bulimic episodes, the place where they occurred, those who were involved before and after the episode, the responses of significant others, the way in which others were helpful or not helpful, her feelings before and after the episode, the foods that she ate (in total), and, finally, the technique of purging. If completed, the journal can be used to determine how others are involved and how the bulimic uses food. The technique often has a paradoxical effect, and the client may not binge and purge for several weeks. Once she returns to the bulimia, however, she should also return to the journal. If the client fails to keep the journal, the therapist should address this issue when exploring the negative consequences of change.

After gathering information, the therapist builds therapeutic realities, frameworks, or themes to challenge the belief system of the couple regarding the bulimia. A therapeutic theme is a palatable idea that can help the couple understand the bulimia in a different way. For example, one theme for eating disorders is commonly built on a developmental reality (Minuchin, 1978). The frame reflects the fact that the eating disorder may be keeping the woman from growing up and becoming an adult. She may

be afraid to grow up, and her spouse may be unsure of who she would be if she became an adult. Other frames may revolve around the bulimia's protective functions, fear of change, conflict phobia, or fear of leaving home. When building therapeutic realities, the therapist uses the characteristics of the couple, the functions of the bulimia, and the information gathered in the sessions. Combining these ingredients, a theme can be constructed that not only challenges the couple, but allows them to feel the support and understanding of the therapist.

Acknowledging the Negative Consequences of Change

During Stage 1, the therapist should routinely assign in-session and between-session tasks to help the couple understand the negative consequences of change. Changing the symptom or altering any of the processes related to the maintenance of the symptom can be very threatening to the couple, as they have not usually considered what they will be giving up if they give up the bulimia. With the therapist's help, however, the client comes to recognize all the ramifications of symptom removal. Establishing these consequences early in the therapeutic process can save the therapist time and energy and may preempt some of the couple's resistance to change.

Either during the session or as a homework assignment, the therapist asks the couple to consider all the risks they would face if they no longer had the protection of the bulimia. Asking the couple to discuss the negative consequences with each other in session, the therapist observes the conversation, comments on the process, and encourages them to explore the risks thoroughly. This intervention is implemented over several sessions, and the outcome information is referred to throughout the therapy.

During the second session, the therapist asked Bob, an alcoholic, and Barb, a bulimic, to write down all the negative consequences they could foresee if they no longer had the bulimia. They were asked to compose separate lists and not to discuss the assignment before the next session. This excerpt is taken from the beginning of the third session.

Therapist (after reading both lists): It is interesting; you both had many of the same negative consequences on your lists. You are both very aware of the risks involved if you no longer have the bulimia and alcohol to cling to. I am impressed with the work you did, and I believe you will be, too. Bob, why don't you begin by sharing one of the scary things on your list?

Bob: Well, you know what you are like after you have thrown up? Well, if you stopped throwing up, you will probably be more social. You might want to go out more and see more people. You know how I feel about going out and big parties.

Barb: Don't worry, Bob, I know how you feel about it, and I won't want to go if you don't want to.

Bob: Then you'll resent me, cause I know how you like parties. Every weekend we will end up in a fight, or you won't talk to me. And if I stop drinking, then I know I won't ever want to be around other people.

Maybe the solution is, you can stop throwing up, and I'll keep drinking. Then we can both have fun at the parties.

This brief interaction supplied the therapist with a wealth of information. The therapist could have chosen to store the information or perhaps to have the couple begin a more in-depth negotiation around the problem of socializing, depending on the goal for that session— either gathering general information or having the couple experience a successful negotiation. This therapist was still attempting to gather information.

Barb: If I stop the bulimia, I will probably have to get a job and maybe even decide about a long-term career. I certainly have been able to avoid that for years because of my moods and my health problems.

Therapist: Bob, what would Barb's working or finding a career mean to you?

Bob: The good would be more money; the bad would be meeting a lot of new people and Barb thinking I was boring and stupid. She would probably have another affair.

Barb: I wouldn't do that to you again. Anyway, maybe therapy will help with your drinking, and then I wouldn't want to be with someone else.

Bob: The time you had the affair was the only time during our marriage that you were not throwing up.

Barb: Maybe therapy can help me so I won't do that.

Bob: That's what I am here for.

When the couple began to recognize patterns and to define the problem of bulimia as a couple's problem, the therapist broadened the intervention to include their families. This helped the couple to understand the effect of the bulimia on their families and the probable impact of symptom removal on their families.

Restraining the Change

Based on the information gathered and the knowledge that people are naturally resistant to change, the therapist may not immediately encourage the client to give up the bulimia. Many clients are relieved to hear that they are not expected to go "cold turkey," but others are disappointed that therapy is not a magic cure. In either situation, because the client, her spouse, and their families have grown dependent on the symptom, a covert power struggle may ensue if the therapist immediately works toward symptom withdrawal. Thus, the therapist begins working in other areas, concurrently monitoring the symptom and helping the couple to see the role that the bulimia plays in their life. A restraining position may also be taken regarding couple interactions other than the bulimia, however.

At the end of the third session with Bob and Barb, the therapist restrained them in regard to their lack of conflict resolution. During the session, the couple discussed the ways in which the bulimia and the alcohol protected them from conflict. If they found themselves in an uncomfortably conflictual situation, they stated that they would go off to their separate corners with their "best friends,"

his being the bottle and hers the food.

Therapist: The two of you just demonstrated to me and to each other that you are capable of resolving conflict, but that you feel safer not attempting to do it. This next week I want you to do something that might sound strange, but is sensible. I want you to continue to avoid conflict and to avoid it the same way you always have.

Barb: What if we have nothing to fight about?

Bob: I am sure we can find something.

Barb (to the therapist): You mean you want me to throw up?

Therapist: I mean, I want you to avoid resolving any conflicts. You both have told me that the change would mean a lot of good and bad things. I do not want you to give up anything until you are clear about the ramifications and the commitment that change involves. You have been fighting and avoiding in this way for a long time. This has become safe for you. The food and the alcohol protect you. Having a new marriage is not going to be easy; it's risky business. I do not want you to take any risks until you are ready.

This intervention obviously may have a paradoxical impact in that the couple may attempt to fight the old way and resolve the conflict without the use of food or alcohol. On the other hand, they may be relieved and, in fact, change nothing.

It is time to move to Stage 2 when

1. a relationship between the therapist and the clients has been established.
2. the role that the bulimia plays in the relationship is relatively clear.
3. the therapist understands the interactional operations that maintain the symptom.
4. a mutually agreed upon language has been created for therapeutic themes.
5. the implications of change are fully understood, and a commitment to change has been made.

Stage 2: Challenging Patterns and Expanding Alternatives

Many couples may begin the second stage of therapy after a few sessions; others, after a few months. The model is designed to be flexible with respect to interventions and pacing. Many interventions overlap into all three stages, and the couple may move between stages from time to time, depending on the content of the case.

Using the information gathered in Stage 1, the therapist raises the intensity level in Stage 2 by promoting conflict and intimacy. The therapist uses the themes that were established in the first stage to challenge the couple and to intervene in dysfunctional patterns. For example, if the couple agreed in Stage 1 that the bulimia keeps the woman young because she returns to her parents' home after an episode and that it protects the husband because he does not experience his own failures, the therapist challenges this sequence by having the couple talk about the pattern or perhaps by involving the families of origin in the sessions. The form of the challenge is determined by the personal preference and style of the therapist.

The logical step to follow the challenge of old patterns is the discovery of alternative behaviors and feelings to replace dysfunctional interactions, particularly those that involve bulimia, with a more flexible process. New ways of functioning in the marriage, with their families, and in the social context are designed by the couple in therapy, with the assistance of the therapist. The therapy enables them to break their rigid views of themselves and others and to be more flexible in their relationships.

The rhythm of therapy changes during this stage, as the therapist participates more actively. Restraining interventions still have a place in Stage 2, but they are not as prominent. They are now used to remind couples of the risk of change and to ease some of the difficult times. After a particularly creative expansion of new interactions, the therapist may predict relapse and restrain the couple from too much change. This produces a comfortable pace for both the couple and the therapist.

In-Session Tasks

The goal of in-session tasks is to produce immediate change in the therapy room. These tasks focus on the couple's communication patterns, providing intense and intimate interactions, and conflict resolution. Most sessions during the second phase of treatment center on the interactions between the couple. The following excerpt is from a Stage 2 session; the therapist was helping to establish the wife as a competent individual.

Therapist: Sue, you have told Steve that you are not so fragile, that he doesn't have to protect you from what goes on in his life. He must not believe you, based on what you have told me he has kept from you in the past few weeks. Are you sure you do not need protecting? Are you sure you are not somehow telling him that you are afraid of what he has to say?

Sue: I used to need protecting. I used to be afraid of everything. Maybe I still am, but I do not want to be. Everyone tries to protect me. Maybe I have to get hurt or be afraid to become strong. But I know I do not want to be protected, if it means my husband can't talk to me.

Therapist: Then convince him you can handle it, convince him to stop parenting you.

Steve: I have to parent you. You even just said you are afraid of everything. You always think I don't love you if I say anything negative. How can I not protect you and not have you think I don't care?

Using the themes that were established in Stage 1, the therapist challenged this couple to change the ideas that they had about one another. Putting the responsibility on them to find new ways of communicating and behaving, the therapist continued to help establish the woman as a strong individual and help persuade the man to give up his role of parenting.

Another in-session intervention may include the families of origin. The therapist should explore the involvement of both families, not just that of the bulimic's family, as both families may have a role in maintaining the symptom. Either set of parents, for example, may take an overprotective and overinvolved role in the marriage during a time of crisis. When members of the extended family attend the session, the goals of treatment remain the same as those for the couple alone—to recognize the function of the symptom and the way in which family members' interactions maintain the problem, to challenge the families' interactional patterns, and to help the extended group discover new avenues to conduct their relationships (Schwartz et al., 1985).

Other in-session tasks focus on the couple's struggles as individuals and the impact of their struggles on the relationship. The individual work may or may not be done in the presence of the spouse. The purpose of these individually oriented sessions is to make each partner more aware of his or her personal conflicts and struggles that affect the other partner and the bulimia. Just as they have never learned to resolve interpersonal conflict, they have never learned to resolve internal conflict. The therapist explores with each his or her history and any crucial events that may never have been explored. During this time, previous abuses or other traumatic events are discussed. In either individual or couple sessions, the therapist helps them to accept the different components in themselves and in one another. Learning from one another about their various personalities is an intimate and eye-opening experience for the couple. In many ways, this therapeutic process for individuals is isomorphic to family sessions.

Between-Session Tasks

Certainly, all the work cannot be done during the sessions. The couple can be assigned tasks to be accomplished outside the therapist's office. The purpose of the between-session tasks is (1) to encourage the couple to work autonomously, (2) to strengthen the continuity of the therapy, (3) to emphasize the content and process of the therapy, and (4) to raise the intensity of work begun in the session. Tasks may focus on the family of origin (Bowen, 1978), or they may be specific interventions designed to have a direct impact on the symptom. These assignments may include communication skills tasks, conflict resolution tasks, or relationship enhancement exercises.

If it is not possible to convene the families of origin or if the therapist prefers not to do so, between-session tasks can be helpful. The couple can be asked to track their families' responses to them and their symptoms. They can log their interactions with one another in the presence of their families, as well as the ways in which their families enter their day-to-day life. In essence, they are asked to gather the information that the therapist would gather if the families attended therapy sessions. Following the information-gathering phase, the tasks focus on helping the couple find new methods to relate to their families. With the help of the therapist, the couple may decide to behave differently at a family gathering, to make fewer telephone calls, or to exclude the parents from any involvement in a bulimic episode. Paradoxically, the couple may be asked to overinvolve the family as a way to help the parents feel more loved and needed. In any case, direct or indirectly, they are asked to challenge and expand the family interactional patterns.

During Stage 2, the bulimic and her spouse are less ambivalent about giving up the symptom. Many times, the symptom has already diminished, even with-

out the use of symptom-specific interventions. If it has not, Stage 2 is the appropriate time to focus on the symptom. The goal may not be the total abolishment of the bulimic behavior, but the elimination of the sequences of thoughts and behaviors that maintain it. The tasks, once again, may be either direct or indirect in nature.

Direct tasks are based on the information obtained from the food journal of Stage 1. Because the bulimic is more aware of the purpose of the bulimia, she can use an episode as a signal. She may be asked to stop before she binges, decide what is the function of the binge, and write down other ways of coping with the situation. Such alternate behaviors include relaxing, finding a source of enjoyment, asserting herself, communicating directly about a difficulty, pushing herself for more intimacy, finding another avenue for privacy, or making a decision independent of her spouse or family. The bulimic may continue the binge-purge sequence after this, but at least there has been a break in an otherwise rigid pattern. Furthermore, she has a choice of behaviors.

Indirect tasks usually involve rituals, ordeals, and/or symptom prescription (Haley, 1985). Many of these tasks exaggerate the interactional sequences in which the bulimic and her spouse are involved. For example, in order to overemphasize the husband's involvement and the implicit struggle for power and control, the therapist may ask the husband to plan, prepare, and direct the binge and purge for his wife (Madanes, 1984). The bulimic may be asked to plan a binge for a particular time during the week, buy the food, prepare it, and throw it away. The intent of these paradoxical tasks is to invoke the couple's resistance to the directive or to intensify their experience around the symptom, thus increasing their control of their behaviors. Tasks are designed both to change the bulimic's rigid behavior and to disrupt the interactional sequences of the couple.

Stage 2 supplied the couple with choices. Recognizing their old patterns and now having new behaviors, thoughts, and feelings to use, they must choose among the options.

Stage 3: Consolidating Changes

The couple must practice and feel comfortable with the changes that they have made and will continue to make. The timing of Stage 3 varies considerably, however, depending on the initial goals of therapy. When the couple no longer uses the therapy session to process problems or resolve conflict, but rather to report the resolution of a stressful situation or the establishment of different boundaries with their families, it is obvious that their need for therapy has been vastly reduced.

The therapist becomes less central during this phase, giving less advice and commenting more on the couple's successes. The couple are asked to look into their crystal ball and predict future trouble areas. These predictions may prevent problems or may simply help the couple to recognize when they are in trouble. Prescribing a relapse or a reenactment of old interactional patterns helps the couple to remain in control of the behaviors that maintained the bulimia; discussion

of their struggles helps them to stay committed to their growth. The interval between sessions becomes greater, but the emphasis on the availability of alternatives in coping with life makes it clear to the couple that therapy is always an option.

Successful outcome may be defined as:

1. a vast reduction in bulimic behavior, but not necessarily total abstinence. Total abstinence from laxative use and abuse is necessary for successful outcome, however.
2. establishment of flexible interactions.
3. a relationship that is not dependent on bulimia for its function.
4. comfortable boundaries, as defined by the couple, between them and their families.
5. more interdependent functioning as a couple.
6. a change in their perceptions of themselves as individuals.

CONCLUSION

Bulimia is a perplexing and frightening disorder. Working with the couple has been shown to be an effective and successful approach to treatment of the disorder. Perhaps because the couple are not as rigidly involved in the patterns that maintain the symptom, they tend to commit to change faster and to exhibit more flexibility. The therapist can easily use this relationship as a vehicle to interrupt the interpersonal, dyadic, and familial patterns involved in the creation and maintenance of bulimia.

REFERENCES

Bepko, C., & Krestan, J. (1985). *The responsibility trap.*

Boskind-White, M., & White, W.C. (1983). *Bulimarexia: The binge/purge cycle.* New York: W.W. Norton.

Bowen, M. (1978). *Family therapy in clinical practice.* New York: Jason Aronson.

Bruch, H. (1973). *Eating disorders: Obesity, anorexia nervosa and the person within.* New York: Basic Books.

Bruch, H. (1978). *The golden cage.* Cambridge, MA: Harvard University Press.

Casper, R. (1983). On the emergence of bulimia nervosa as a syndrome. *International Journal of Eating Disorders*

Fisch, R., Weakland, J., & Segal, L. (1982). *The tactics of change.* San Francisco: Jossey-Bass.

Garner, D.M., & Garfinkel, P.E. (1985). *Handbook of psychotherapy for anorexia nervosa and bulimia.* New York: Guilford Press.

Haley, J. (1976). *Problem solving therapy.* San Francisco: Jossey-Bass.

Haley, J. (1985). *Ordeal therapy.* San Francisco: Jossey-Bass.

Madanes, C. (1984). *Strategic family therapy.* San Francisco: Jossey-Bass.

Minuchin, S. (1974). *Families and family therapy.* Cambridge, MA: Harvard University Press.

Minuchin, S., & Fishman, H.C. (1981). *Family therapy techniques.* Cambridge, MA: Harvard University Press.

Minuchin, S., Rosman, B., & Baker, L. (1978). *Psychosomatic families: Anorexia nervosa in context.* Cambridge, MA: Harvard University Press.

Saba, G., Barrett, M.J., & Schwartz, R. (1983). All or nothing: The bulimic epidemic. *Family Therapy Networker, 7,* 43–44.

Schwartz, R.C. (1986). *Intrapsychic process revisited: A systemic model of internal family therapy.* Unpublished manuscript.

Schwartz, R., Barrett, M.J., & Saba, G. (1985). Family therapy for bulimia. In D. Garner & P. Garfinkel (Eds.), *Handbook for psychotherapy for anorexia nervosa and bulimia* (pp. 280–310). New York: Guilford Press.

Schwartz, R., Barret, M.J. & Saba, G. (In Press). *Systemic treatment of bulimia.* New York: Guilford Press.

Selvini-Palazzoli, M., Boscolo, L., Cecchin, G. & Prata, G. (1978). *Paradox and counterparadox.* New York: Jason Aronson.

4

Brief Therapy and Eating Disorders

Vincent A. Moley, MA
Director
Eating Disorders Center
Mental Research Institute
Palo Alto, California

THE MRI BRIEF THERAPY model is a goal-oriented, directive, time-limited model of interpersonal therapy. In essence, it involves the use of cybernetic principles to delineate the factors that maintain a given symptom or problem. These problem-maintaining patterns are operationally defined as the pseudo-solutions that the system (individual and interpersonal) has been applying to the problem. In addition, the brief therapist aims to understand the function that the symptom/problem serves for the system. Once the function of the symptom is understood, the therapist not only can help the system to achieve the same function at less cost to itself, but also can preempt relapse. Therefore, the primary goals of treatment are to interrupt the pseudo-solutions and enable the system to develop a new pattern of organization.

BRIEF THERAPY APPROACH TO EATING DISORDERS

From the viewpoint of brief therapy theory and practice, eating disorders arise from everyday difficulties associated with certain developmental stages of the individual and family life cycle. These disorders are maintained by the pseudo-solutions implemented by the clients themselves and others, including family members. The majority of clients seen at the MRI Eating Disorders Center are women.

In working with eating disorders or any other problem, the brief therapist aims primarily to:

- obtain a clear description of the chief complaint

- identify the pseudo-solutions of the client and others
- interrupt these pseudo-solutions
- achieve small changes in the problem and amplify these changes
- manage relapses

To these ends, therapy sessions are used for data collection, behavioral prescriptions, and reframings. In order to facilitate these processes, family members are frequently seen separately.

The foci of change are the client's actions in relation to the problem *outside* the therapy session. The therapist functions as a problem solver during sessions, using influence and persuasion. Consistent with its nonnormative orientation, brief therapy is terminated when the clients have achieved their goals rather than when the therapist has normalized the presumed pathology. Overall, the brief therapist is guided by two principles: "If it works, do not fix it." and "Let sleeping dogs lie."

There is no simple formula for the successful treatment of eating disorders, but there are some common patterns. For example, parents and other family members are likely to be directly involved in the treatment of young clients with eating disorders. Treatment is typically terminated after 7 to 15 sessions. Early sessions are conducted weekly; middle sessions, biweekly; and ending sessions, on a variable schedule. Follow-up interviews are conducted with clients 6 months, 12 months, and 18 months after the final session.

INTERACTIONAL VIEW OF EATING DISORDERS

From a theoretical perspective, eating disorders are developed and maintained at the intersection of three levels: the societal, the interpersonal/familial, and the individual.

Societal Context of Eating Disorders

Over the last 25 years, the idealized body type for women has become progressively more slender (Palazzoli, 1985). Accompanying this idealization of slimness has been the construction of a social taboo against fatness. Society associates positive attributes of attractiveness, self-discipline, health, education, moral virtue, youth, and excellence with slimness, while associating diametrically opposed attributes with fatness. Furthermore, this taboo against fatness exists within a contemporary societal trend of conformity that counters, for example, the value placed on diversity and protest in the 1960s.

Unfortunately, the prescribed route to slender conformity is dieting, which appears to be a strategy of weight control and body shape modification that may exacerbate the very problem it is intended to solve (Bennett & Gurin, 1982; Harkaway, 1983; Moley, 1983). Taken together, these factors create a context in which many women are likely to develop eating disorders. A neglected area of research is the precise way in which most women avoid eating disorders or, having developed them, stop using them.

From a brief therapy perspective, the general increase in the incidence of eating disorders (e.g., anorexia nervosa, bulimia, and compulsive overeating) is linked to the societal definition of fatness as a problem and the promotion of dieting as a solution to this socially constructed problem (Moley, 1983). The maintenance of a given individual's eating disorder is understood in terms of the pseudo-solutions applied to it by that individual and others. In addition, a relapse in an eating disorder is believed to result from the function that the disorder serves in an individual and interpersonal context.

Interpersonal/Familial Context of Eating Disorders

Because of their public nature, certain eating disorders, in particular self-starvation, become functional in interpersonal conflicts. The familial developmental stage that corresponds to adolescence in the offspring inevitably involves multiple conflicts, for example; if a family member develops an eating disorder in such a context, the family may abandon alternate paths of conflict resolution and establish a coherent, self-maintaining interactional pattern around the eating behavior. In this view, familial styles of interaction and conflict management co-evolve with the individual eating disorder.

Self-starvation may represent an adolescent's extreme form of defiance against his or her parents, sometimes a struggle until death. In this case, self-starvation within the family mirrors the strategy of the hunger strikes that political protesters use when they perceive more conventional or more violent power strategies as unavailable or unacceptable. In order to be effective, such strategies require a split in the opposition, some members of which must be in sympathy with the self-starvers so that, even if the starvers die, they may at least win a moral victory and further split the opposition. Interestingly, as early as the 19th century,

clinicians have observed that the parents of anorectics may unwittingly exacerbate their offspring's symptom by dissension. In 1873, Lasegue noted that anorectics had a poor prognosis if their parents alternated between "entreaties and menaces" in trying to influence their offspring. In addition, these parents created a context in which the anorectic became the sole preoccupation of the family, imbuing the self-starver with even more power (Lasegue, 1964).

While self-starvation may represent a form of defiance within the family, it also represents a form of extreme compliance with societal ideals and taboos. Similarly, the other eating disorders can be understood as dimensions of defiance and compliance. For example, if known to the parents, a daughter's bingeing and purging may represent a defiance of her parents, somewhat analogous to throwing temper tantrums; at the same time, her concern with body weight conforms to societal ideals. If the bingeing and purging is conducted in secret, however, the daughter is usually compliant with both family and societal norms. Typically, the secret bulimic or compulsive overeater is more interested in treatment than is the anorectic or public bulimic. In the latter cases, it is usually the parents who seek help.

Just as a young girl may become addicted to the experience of self-starvation, bingeing and purging, or compulsive overeating, her parents may become "addicted" to their self-defeating attempts to change their daughter's behavior. All parties obtain short-term relief from distress, but they find themselves in a worse predicament that requires more relief. The parents believe that, although their efforts have not been successful, at least they are doing "the right thing" and they should try even harder. The daughter escapes the difficulties of everyday life through her eating disorder and achieves a Pyrrhic victory in the face of her parent's attempts to control her. Such interactional escalations, like wars, are notoriously easy to start and difficult to end, because the declaration of such strategies preempts other paths to conflict resolution (Moley, 1985).

A third party or therapist may resolve such conflicts in two ways: (1) by empowering one party to obtain the unconditional surrender of the adversary (i.e., the structural approach, which empowers the parents vis-a-vis their child) or (2) by using diplomacy from a position of neutrality (i.e., the brief therapy approach). The brief therapist uses diplomacy to reach a negotiated settlement in a context of mutual self-interest (Moley, 1985).

Individual Context of Eating Disorders

Eating disorders may be maintained by both the physiological and psychological processes of the individual. The onset of most eating disorders can be traced to a period of excessive dieting. Such dieting typically followed either the natural weight gain concomitant with puberty or a later weight gain that drew criticism from peers or family members. Excessive dieting can disrupt certain physiological homeostatic processes that control body fat (Keesey & Corbett, 1983).

The strategy of dieting for weight loss in the long term is self-defeating in a number of ways. First, it can lead to a reduction in the basic metabolic rate; second, the individual actually loses lean muscle tissue and water before losing fat. Thus, the resumption of normal eating, combined with a slowed metabolic rate, may actually increase the proportion of fat in body weight composition. These factors, in part, account for the fact that people who rely on episodic dieting for weight control often show a progressively increased body weight over their lifetime. The most successful strategies for weight loss involve a combination of increased physical activity and a moderate reduction in calorie intake.

Excessive dieting may also affect cognitive and behavioral patterns. For example, normal volunteers put on starvation diets experienced virtually all the classic symptoms of anorexia nervosa, including social isolation, depression, preoccupation with food, obsessiveness, and difficulty with attention and concentration (Garfinkel & Gardner, 1982; Keys, Brozek, Henschel, Mickelsen, & Taylor, 1950). In fact, self-starvation appears to lead to a state of self-intoxication. While most people find this state of intoxication unpleasant, others find it a welcome relief from the troubles of everyday life. From this perspective, anorexia nervosa can be seen as a form of chronic self-intoxication.

Bulimia creates a self-intoxication that is more episodic and less intense than that of anorexia nervosa. Typically, the bulimic relieves boredom, anxiety, or stress through bingeing; panics at the thought of weight gain; and purges, experiencing short-term relief and a "twilight" psychological state. This series of events is followed by a sense of guilt and defeat, and the pattern is repeated.

The self-intoxication of compulsive overeating is less dramatic and more tranquilizing than that of self-starvation or bulimia. In the self-maintaining cycle of overeating, the individual feels sad and defeated by his or her weight gain, eats to experience solace, then feels even more demoralized, and eats more. Taken together, therefore, the psychological experiences associated with eating disorders are similar to those of any addiction.

TREATMENT

Compulsive overeating, bingeing and purging, and self-starvation serve progressively higher functions in the context of interpersonal conflict and as a form of self-intoxication. A given individual may move up and down this continuum at different developmental life stages. A shift from one eating disorder to another represents a first-order change. The goal of treatment is to effect a second-order change by interrupting the pattern of pseudo-solutions vis-a-vis the eating disorder and to enable the individual to resolve conflict and relieve psychological distress in less harmful ways.

Anorexia Nervosa

Typically, it is the parents of the anorectic who seek help. If the anorectic, most often a daughter, comes to the first interview at all, she usually does so under considerable duress. The resulting intense, unresolved, and unspoken conflict between the parents and the daughter interferes with the brief therapy task of problem definition and data gathering. Therefore, the warring parties are often seen separately, and the therapist typically tries to influence the daughter through the parents.

In interviewing the parents, the therapist presumes that they are doing the best they can in difficult circumstances. After questioning the parents about their attempted solutions, the therapist gives directives designed to interrupt them, making these directives consistent with the parents' language and their view of their daughter's problem. If the parents disagree about the best way to help their daughter, the therapist says that these differences are understandable and reframes the conflict. For example, the therapist may point out that the parents agree on the ultimate goals for their daughter (i.e., that she be healthy), but disagree about the means to achieve this goal. Such a reframing defines a larger context of accord and relegates the parental conflict to a minor disagreement about tactics. As the parents develop more confidence in their ability to help their daughter, the parental conflicts frequently resolve spontaneously.

In the reframing intervention, the therapist may state to the parents:

> You are clearly very intimidated by your daughter's symptom. Your daughter is aware of this and thereby experiences a great deal of power over you. While it is useful for her to begin to experience power over adults, she experiences so much power over you that she is extremely frightened. Therefore, you need to reassure her that she does not have that much power by acting *as if* you are not as intimidated by her behavior. You can do this by acknowledging together to her that you will never be able to get her to eat against her will and by suggesting that you may have been bad parents in trying to make her eat. You then add that, because she is ill from malnutrition, she should stay in bed and that, if she gets any weaker, you will have to take her to a hospital. This will be not only for her own safety, but also for your own peace of mind and perception of yourselves as parents.

Such an approach on behalf of the parents introduces complementarity into the symmetrical struggle between the parents and their daughter.

Conducting interviews with the anorectic daughter is difficult for two reasons. First, the daughter often perceives the therapist as an agent of the parents. Second, when the daughter is severely malnourished, she is in such a state of self-intoxication that communication is very limited.

In the interview with the anorectic, the therapist may explain the toxic effects of starvation in normal volunteers, implying that she may have unwittingly poisoned herself in her attempts to lose weight. The therapist may suggest that, while no one can force her to eat, she should seek medical attention so that she can decide what she wants to do with a clear head. If the patient complains that she has no desire to eat, the therapist may explain that this is understandable and predictable in view of her condition, that at this stage food should be seen as fuel, and that the desire for and pleasure in food will come in the future.

Once the anorectic is more aware, the therapist may point out that the strategy of self-starvation is counterproductive in her struggle with her parents, because they can discount anything she does or says on the ground that she is "crazy." In addition, it is often useful to reframe her behavior as helpful to the parents in that she is distracting them from other problems and conflicts. If the anorectic is older, the therapist may define the anorectic's role as that of both scapegoat and martyr to her family. Because of these roles, she has learned something rather unique and special about social processes. She may be cautioned that,

while this knowledge makes her somewhat exceptional among her peers, she should be careful in the future about her tendency to sacrifice herself to distract others from painful conflicts.

The key to success in the treatment of anorexia is correcting the toxic effects of anorexia, which may require hospitalization and medical supervision. Relapse may be preempted through prescription and interruption of the parents' pattern of attempted solutions.

Bulimia

Like the anorectic, the public bulimic is often uninterested in treatment. The parent-bulimic conflict is usually more direct than is the parent-anorectic conflict, and the parents of the bulimic feel less intimidated by the symptom. Moreover, other family members may be in open conflict with the bulimic because of stolen family food and malodorous bathrooms.

One bulimic daughter had taken to storing vomit in her room to such a degree that the family home constantly reeked of vomit. The daughter also threw her containers of vomit into the garbage, which so annoyed the sanitation workers that they adopted the passive-aggressive strategy of leaving vomit strewn through the backyard and garden.

In situations such as this, the parents are often amenable to taking direct concerted actions.

Escalations in public bulimia may be very dramatic.

A daughter who lived with her divorced mother would eat all the food from the refrigerator and then vomit it. At one point, the mother put a chain around the refrigerator handle, but the food continued to disappear, leading the mother to question her own sanity. One day, the refrigerator leaked water, and the mother called a repairman. He found that someone had been removing and replacing the refrigerator door to get past the chain. After this incident, the mother moved the food, except flour and milk, to a neighbor's house. The daughter proceeded to make massive quantities of pancakes from these staples for her binges. Finally, the mother moved all the food to her neighbor's house, whereupon the daughter broke into the neighbor's house to get the food.

Thus, the mother had implemented an escalating range of attempted solutions (i.e., keeping food away), which predictably maintained the problem. The therapist intervened by instructing the mother and daughter to shop together each week for the food on which the daughter would binge during the following week. The mother was to make sure that the daughter was eating the food. The daughter was discouraged from vomiting, but encouraged to binge and keep copious notes on her inner experiences. The daughter rapidly ceased her bingeing. The mother and the daughter became embroiled in some very realistic conflicts that were resolved by the daughter's leaving home successfully. Meanwhile, the mother directed her attention to her own social and professional life.

In this case, the mother's attempted solutions were interrupted by directing her to encourage her daughter's bingeing. The daughter's attempted solutions, trying not to think of bingeing and resolving never to binge again, were interrupted by encouraging planned binges. Finally, by defining the binges as cooperative acts between mother and daughter, the therapist deprived them of their function as a symbol of conflict and autonomy.

Treatment of the secret bulimic is essentially the same as treatment of the compulsive overeater.

Compulsive Overeating

Usually older than anorectics or public bulimics, compulsive overeaters are more likely to be self-referred for treatment. The focus of brief therapy is typically the client's attempted solutions and the interpersonal consequences of change.

In some cases, the overeating may be associated with parental efforts to get their daughter to lose weight by putting her on diets, sending her to "fat farms," supervising her meals, cajoling, threatening, or even ridiculing her. Such strategies may be counterproductive in a number of ways. For example, the dieting may disrupt the self-regulation of body weight and appetite, or the daughter may come to use body weight as an expression of independence and rebelliousness.

The consequences of compulsive overeating and, thus, overweight may not become evident until the daughter is older. At this point, the interpersonal conflicts are often linked to peer group members or spouses rather than to the family of origin.

Compulsive overeaters use food as a source of pleasure, solace, and distraction in the same way that others use moderate amounts of alcohol or tobacco. Social overeating is usually more controlled and less personally distressing than is solitary "emotional overeating." In the latter case, the individual is likely to use food to alleviate the unpleasant emotional states associated with interpersonal conflicts, including loneliness. Although the individual is likely to gain short-term relief from distress, the long-term result may be progressive withdrawal from life conflicts and problems.

The brief therapy approach to compulsive overeating and secret bulimia involves the simultaneous pursuit of two goals: (1) elucidation of the client's attempted solutions to overeating and weight gain with a view to change and (2) exploration of the functions of the symptom with a view to relapse management and recovery. While attempted solutions may vary with each case, common self-defeating strategies involve:

- trying to fight the desire to eat
- adopting an "all or nothing" approach (e.g., "I am never going to overeat again.")
- dieting
- keeping tempting foods outside the home
- trying not to think of food
- searching for some magical solution or pill.

These strategies are countered by the position of neutrality that the therapist takes vis-a-vis weight. For example, the therapist may say, "Why would you want to stop overeating? It's a source of pleasure in your life." The therapist may also play the role of devil's advocate, emphasizing the negative consequences or dangers of change.

The client is at first instructed not to change. She is told to binge as much as she wants, but to keep notes of what she eats and her inner experiences around eating. She is also instructed to list both the negative and positive consequences of change, particularly in terms of her interpersonal relationships. The client can be encouraged to have a planned binge to explore further the functions of bingeing and/or to postpone minor binges so that she can experience a major spontaneous binge.

If the client completes the note-taking assignment, she can then be advised to begin a regime of moderate exercise—while continuing to eat as much as she wants. She should record and differentiate the eating she does for fuel and nourishment from the eating she does for emotional reasons. She is encouraged to think about food and to desire food as much as she wants, but to consider basing her pleasure experiences on quality rather than on quantity. The client is encouraged not to fight the desire, but to postpone action. *Technically,* it is possible to postpone a binge for days, months, or even years. Such a reframing avoids the "all or nothing" approach and "finality or loss" of never bingeing again. Thus, by using the strategy of restraining, the therapist encourages the client to think small and change slowly.

If the client does not carry out the note-taking assignment, the therapist moves to the strategy of restraint. The therapist points out that the client probably has too much on her plate to give her problem the undivided attention that it requires. Avoiding a struggle with the client, the therapist notes that she does not have to change, that she may not be ready for change yet, and that the benefits of this problem for others obviously outweigh the costs to herself. The therapist may point out that it is not possible to help her achieve the same functions at less cost to herself without determining the real functions. Conjectures during the session as to potential functions can be discounted as distorted self-report. The real functions can be determined only by notes taken at the time of the binge. The client at this stage has three choices:

1. postpone treatment until she is ready to take notes
2. carry out the assignment
3. not binge as a way to avoid taking notes.

The first choice keeps the client from wasting her own and the therapist's time. The other choices begin to change the problem.

In suggesting that overeating or overweight serves a function, the therapist shifts the meaning of the symptom from that of an uncontrollable habit or addiction to that of a purposeful activity over which the client has at least potential influence. This reframing also enables the therapist to shift the self-attributions of the client from those of badness, lack of self-discipline, and laziness to those of benevolent self-sacrifice and protection of others. For example, a client may report that the function of her symptom is to keep her uninvolved with romantic and sexual partners. The therapist accepts this and extends it:

> It is clear that you have a phobia against rejecting men. If you could not convince yourself that you are unattractive, you would have men approaching you, some of whom you would find undesirable. As you are very sensitive to men's feelings, you would have difficulty rejecting them; thus, you would unwittingly hurt both yourself and them in the longer term. Therefore, you need to desensitize yourself to rejecting men before you lose weight.

The stage is now set for social activity, portrayed as a behavioral experiment rather than a desperate search for acceptance. In addition, the client can act as if she already were as she wishes to be. Acting "as if," particularly in a social context, can introduce randomness into the compulsive overeater's redundant life style (Watzlawick, 1985). New interpersonal experiences can also provide a distraction from the client's intense preoccupation with food and weight.

It is usually possible to achieve small changes in eating behavior quite early in treatment. The task then becomes the management of relapses. When relapses occur, the client is likely to discount the changes that she has achieved, believing that nothing has really changed, that the disease has taken over her life again, and that she is powerless. However, relapses can be prescribed and reframed. Small relapses can be prescribed as an opportunity to study the function of the symptom further. Spontaneous relapses can be cast as similar opportunities, as well as a means of slowing progress that is too rapid. The client can be instructed to welcome small spontaneous relapses and to plan a small relapse if she does not experience one spontaneously.

The therapist may also use theatrical prescriptions to explore the function of the symptom. In these cases, the therapist explains that the client can achieve the same results provided by the symptom by pretending to have the symptom of overeating and by minimizing her weight loss to others. Alternately, the client may be instructed to feign mild depression or distress in other areas of her life. Such activities not only mediate the interpersonal rebound effects of change, but also maintain the protective function of the symptom for both the client and others.

FAMILY TREATMENT OF SELF-STARVATION

Liza was a 30-year-old single woman who lived alone and worked part-time as a library assistant. She had moved out of the family home less than 1 year ago and had daily contact with her parents. Her younger sister had successfully left home at late adolescence and lived out of state. She sought treatment because of difficulties at work and concerned reactions of colleagues and her parents to her extremely emaciated appearance. Following standard procedure at the Eating Disorder Center, the client was required to have a medical consultation to rule out any medical reasons for her emaciated state as well as to determine the potential medical consequences of her state of malnutrition. At the time of the first interview, Liza weighed 79 lbs. She was 5 feet, 4 inches tall.

The major interventions with Liza were:

1. reframing her experience of anxiety and distress as a result of her unwitting self-intoxication
2. using analogy and metaphor to shift her perception of her body from that of adversary to that of dependent
3. restraining change through a variety of slowing interventions.

The main interventions with the family were:

1. interrupting the parents' attempted solutions vis-a-vis their daughter's self-starvation by instructing them not to encourage her to eat more, but to check that she was not eating too much
2. shifting attention from past resentments to current and future conflicts
3. suggesting that the parents and daughter be less polite to each other and instead be more direct and specific in their criticisms of each other.

The client was seen alone at the first session.

Session #1

Therapist: What's the problem that you want help from us with?

Liza: What I want to do is to have an image of myself as being a nice looking person. I think of myself as 25 lbs heavier than what I am. I would like to be able to relax, to be in control. What I do is this: I watch all day long very carefully what I eat and, as the hours go on, I feel safer and safer to put more down. I figure, "Well. . . ," But, you see, I'm afraid I'm going to lose control and start overeating and so that way I'll get fat. Because when I was a little girl I used to always be overweight. So, of course, everybody wants to be thin, right? So when I was around age 13 I was always on diets. I never did anything really crazy then.

Therapist: In my experience, people who have problems with self-starvation are experts in nutrition.

Liza: I know what I'm supposed to eat. I *know* what's good for me. But I've always had to watch what I ate. My younger sister was always thin and could eat what she wanted. I was always a little pudgy, a few pounds overweight.

Therapist: How much do you weigh now?

Liza: I guess I'm in the low 80s. I'm 5 feet, 4 inches. I've weighed 80 lbs for about 1 year.

Therapist: So in terms of the problem that you are having right now, what would like from us?

Liza: Possibly to put on the weight, but I guess I'd have to feel there is a certain amount of control. That I can control myself. I don't know if I should be letting loose and let someone else control me or whether I need to control myself. And that is the conflict. It's control. How much control do I have. For instance, with my family. I moved out of the house only last year, 29 years old. I was ashamed to be 29 years old and live in the house, and I would sort of hide that. Maybe I was so insecure . . . I still am. But I had a job. I had somewhere to go, and I was using all my creative abilities. But now I don't like myself, I don't like the way I look, I don't like to be around people, I don't like their reaction to me. They look frightened and seem to think I look weird. In a sense, when, for example, the people at work come in, I laugh, you know. But the problem is that I don't feel comfortable starting out the day eating enough. I'm afraid I'll lose control.

Interviewing Liza was somewhat difficult because, as is common with many self-starvers, her speech and thinking were somewhat confused. She expressed a high degree of resentment toward people, combined with a self-righteous stance of "It's me against the world." The therapist pointed out the effects of self-starvation on normal volunteers, and Liza could relate very directly to the cognitive and behavioral consequences. In a sense, the therapist's discussion of this theme normalizes and depathologizes the client in suggesting that she may have arrived at this somewhat deranged state unwittingly in her attempts to lose weight. The rest of the session was concerned with gaining Liza's commitment to continued medical assessment.

The therapist began to engage Liza in an analogy by asking if she had ever had a very young pet or intended to have a baby in the future. Liza replied that she had had a kitten to which she had been very attached. The therapist pointed out that a kitten is very dependent on its owner to provide its basic means of life support and that, if the owner does not take care of it, the kitten can cause a great deal of trouble—not out of maliciousness, but simply out of anxiety, fear, and helplessness. Liza agreed. The therapist then asked Liza to imagine that she had a can of cat food marked poison and asked if she would feed it to her pet. Liza answered vehemently, "No." The therapist said, "That's interesting, because the relationship that you have with your body is exactly the same as that between an owner and a young kitten. While you need your body to experience the pleasure of life, your body is very trusting. For your body, self-starvation is poison."

This analogy is derived from hypnotic work with habit control (Spiegel & Spiegel, 1978). Its usefulness with self-starvers is that it can shift the seeming symmetrical struggle between mind and body to a complementary relationship, in which the mind is defined as more powerful than, and therefore responsible for, the body. From this perspective, the therapist defined food as fuel and nourishment, and as a tranquilizer that could enable Liza to feel more comfortably relaxed.

The next session was scheduled with the parents and Liza together.

Session #2

Liza's parents were in their mid-60s. The therapist adopted a present and future orientation to conflict resolution, pointing out that, in their politeness toward her, the parents were treating their daughter as someone who was extremely fragile.

The therapist interrupted a distracting and confusing interaction of accusation-defense between the daughter and parents concerning her resentment about her childhood:

Therapist: But *now* you want to get over this. Would it be OK with you, Liza, if your parents were to treat you as less fragile? Maybe a little more roughly? Could you take it?

Liza: (*laughing*) Sure. That would be OK.

Therapist: (*to Liza*) You were saying that your parents were treating you as

very fragile as you were growing up. (*to parents*) And you were treating her as if she were fragile for a very good reason, because she was fragile.

Mother: She was very sensitive.

Therapist: Well, very sensitive, yes. But let me ask you a question (*to Liza*). When you no longer have this problem with self-starvation, what will you be faced with then?

Liza: Hmmm . . . good question. I have a partial answer and that is that, if it's not one thing, it's probably something else. Toward my family, the resentment that is deep might come out. I resent the fact that we could never do things together. That is when we would argue: when holidays came around and how we were going to spend the little money we had to spend.

Therapist: So it's the resentment. (*to mother*) Would you prefer she were honest about this or that she be deceptive and keep it inside?

Mother: I prefer she be honest. I know it's there.

Father: I'd rather she were honest, too. One hundred percent honest.

Therapist: So if she has a resentment, she should express it.

Mother: That way she could express her anger. She has a lot of anger. Since she was a child.

Therapist: (*to Liza*) So they want you to express it effectively in whatever way you can effectively express it. And the other question is that you are saying that the next thing you'll be facing when you are over this self-starvation is effectively expressing frustration and anger toward your family. That's in relation to your family. How about in relation to the rest of the world?

Liza: Well, that's in relation to the rest of the world, too. For example, that's what was happening on the job. I feel I took lots of years of being dominated. (*Mother agrees.*)

Therapist: (to Liza) So the next problem you'll face is being more assertive?

Liza: Yes, I have to be more assertive. Not to be afraid that I'm going to fail. That's hard.

Therapist: Because we were thinking about how you are going to deal with that, will your parents help you or not. Especially with your eating. It's very clear that you have a phobia about fatness and also a phobia about losing control. A mental condition: fear. You have a fear that you will just keep on putting on weight and then you will just keep blowing up like a Michelin balloon.

Father: To just put it in one word, she needs a coach, right?

Therapist: I think that you might be onto something interesting there, but this kind of coaching would be along the lines of coaching her to slow down. So your role, both of you (*parents*), would be in relation to Liza saying, "Are you sure you are not eating too much? Slow down." Because her fear is that she is going to lose control and eat too much.

Liza: That's true.

Therapist: (*to parents*) So you can really help her by restraining rather than encouraging her to eat. "Don't do that because that will make you, Liza, feel more out of control." (*to Liza*) What you need is your parents to discourage you from eating too much. (*to parents*) To almost make sure that she is not eating too much.

Mother: Slow her down?

Therapist: Yes.

Father: Now. Suppose there is a lot of food on the table that are only vegetables. There are no calories in them. It's like nothing. So suppose I were to suggest to her to eat food that had more calories in it.

Therapist: No, no. Because her fear is that she is going to lose control, so if you encourage her to eat different sorts of foods, then that is making her feel more panicked. So what you actually need to do is to suggest to her that she slow down. Remind her, coach her, to slow down, not to eat too much too fast. What I'm saying is that she has a phobia about putting on weight. When you are dealing with a person who is afraid of bridges, you don't tell them, "Well, cross that bridge." You hold their hand, you walk with them a step at a time and reassure them not to walk too fast across that bridge, not to feel too uncomfortable. What I'm asking you to do is to almost reverse what you've been doing up to now: you've been encouraging her to eat. I'm asking you to coach her, to reassure her that you are going to make sure that she doesn't get out of control. Are you prepared to do that?

Father: Could you tell us a sort of program?

Therapist: OK. A program would be. . . . You are cooking all the meals for your parents, no?

Liza: Yes.

Mother: But she doesn't eat them.

Father: That's correct.

Therapist: (*to parents*) She cooks them, and you eat. What I'm asking you to do is to discourage her from doing that cooking.

Mother: (*laughing*) Good-bye.

Therapist: Now, when she comes over, she can cook only 25 percent. Another thing is, when she comes around, make sure to tell her, "I hope you haven't been eating too much."

Mother: That seems strange to say.

Therapist: It will seem strange, but you understand the rationale for it, don't you? She has a fear, and you can help her by holding her hand and making sure she doesn't eat too much. Will you do that?

Mother: It's hard to do.

Therapist: It's hard to do. I'm not saying it's easy. But we are now getting a more clear idea of what the problem is, and the problem is this psychological phobia about putting on weight too quickly. And you don't need to be pushed across this bridge; you need to do it at a pace that's comfortable for you.

Liza: The other day my parents were talking about some food that they couldn't stand, that they really didn't like to eat, and I began to salivate.

Liza's last statement provides some confirmation of the view that her parents' attempted solution of encouraging her to eat is counterproductive.

In this case, the treatment continued along the theme of getting Liza's parents to stop encouraging her not only to eat, but also to want to eat. The parents, seen separately for a number of sessions, were given assignments along similar lines. Liza, also seen separately, was encouraged to eat slowly and to think about the problems that she would face when she no longer had this problem. Most of these problems centered around interpersonal conflicts.

The starvation state was characterized as a form of self-intoxication, and Liza was encouraged to go through withdrawal slowly, but progressively. Altogether, the treatment course extended through 12 sessions.

Follow-up Interview

Six months later, Liza came in for a follow-up interview. Her treatment goals had been to feel comfortable weighing 105 lbs and not to feel totally out of control about her eating.

Therapist: How bad have things been?

Liza: I'm doing quite well. I think I'm seeing the possibility of changing my image about myself. I'm at another stage in which I'm trying to deal with what I am right now, to really see it, and it's hard. I'm trying to associate with what I look like rather than being obsessed about what I'm putting down my throat.

Therapist: How much do you weigh now?

Liza: I think I'm 100 or 103 lbs. I also have changed the clothes I wear. I'm starting to wear more clothes that will show what I really look like. I'm also adjusting clothes to a bigger size and not freaking out. I still am not very comfortable in certain social situations where food is available; I don't know whether I'm going to go wild or what. I still don't trust myself totally in those situations. I have not quite figured that one out, yet.

Therapist: It takes a while to learn to trust oneself. Don't rush into it.

Liza: When I get nervous in social situations now, I just go out and get some fresh air. I just go for a walk, and that is no trouble whatsoever. It seems to work. I'm still trying to relax. Now I want to understand what I'm feeling, what I'm looking like, and I'm trying to move really slowly. I think I know what the right pace is.

Liza's strong position of resentment vis-a-vis her family and the world had evaporated. Rather than defining herself

as a victim, she now saw herself as an active participant in her experiences and state. This change seems to be related to her improved state of nutrition and her self-generated capacity to handle conflicts more effectively.

Liza was seen for another interview 6 months later. In the interim period, she had experienced a brief relapse; this relapse had coincided with organizational changes and conflicts at her work. She was able to correct her self-starvation and had changed jobs. At this point, Liza had much less frequent contact with her parents and was more active socially.

In common with some anorectics, Liza may have a longer term tendency to engage in self-starvation when faced with interpersonal conflict. Although there may be little she can do about this tendency, there is a great deal she can do about the *expression* of this tendency.

REFERENCES

Bennett, W., & Gurin, J. (1982). *The dieter's dilemma: Eating less and weighing more.* New York: Basic Books.

Garfinkel, P., & Gardner, D. (1982). *Anorexia nervosa: A multidimensional perspective.* New York: Brunner/Mazel.

Harkaway, J. (1983). Obesity: Reducing the larger system. *Journal of Strategic and Systemic Therapy, 2*(3), 2–15.

Keesey, R.E., & Corbett, S.W. (1983). Metabolic defense of the body-weight set point. *Psychiatric Anals, 13*(11), 839–842.

Keys, A., Brozek, J., Henschel, A., Mickelsen, O., & Taylor, H.L. (1950). *The biology of human starvation.* Minneapolis: University of Minnesota Press.

Lasegue, E.C. (1964). On hysterical anorexia. In M.R. Kaufman & M. Heiman (Eds.), *Evolution*

of psychosomatic concepts (pp. 141–155). New York: International Universities Press. (Original work published in 1873)

Moley, V.A. (1983). Interactional treatment of eating disorders. *Journal of Strategic and Systemic Therapy, 2* (4).

Moley, V.A. (1985). An interactional view of international disorders. *Journal of Strategic and Systemic Therapy, 4*(2), 70–76.

Palazzoli, M.S. (1985). Anorexia nervosa: A syndrome of the affluent society. *Journal of Strategic and Systemic Therapy, 4* (3), 12–16.

Spiegel H., & Spiegel, D. (1978). *Trance and treatment: Clinical uses of hypnosis.* New York: Basic Books.

Watzlawick, P. (1985). If you desire to see, learn how to act. Paper presented at the *Evolution of Psychotherapy Conference,* Phoenix, Arizona, Dec. 12.

5

Ordering a Therapeutic Context: A Developmental Interactional Approach to the Treatment of Eating Disorders in a College Counseling Center

Linda L. Terry, EdD
Assistant Professor, Coordinator
  Marriage and Family Therapy
  Program
Graduate and Continuing Education
Fairfield University
Fairfield, Connecticut

T HE TREATMENT OF BULIMIA and compulsive eating in a college counseling center requires a consideration both of the behavioral processes that characterize these eating disorders and of the unique aspects of mental health services provided in a campus environment. While the family therapy literature has indicated the usefulness of examining eating disorder behavior in its appropriate social context (Minuchin, Rosman, & Baker, 1978; Moley, 1983; Selvini-Palazzoli, 1974), the college counseling literature has focused on such behavior only in an individual context.

The increasing incidence of eating disorders on college campuses, particularly bulimia and compulsive eating, has been widely reported (Boskind-Ledahl & White, 1978; Boskind-White & White, 1983; Halmi, Falk, & Schwartz, 1981; Katzman & Wolchik, 1984; Neuman & Halvorson, 1983; Weinstein & Richman, 1984). Halmi, Falk, and Schwartz (1981) estimated that 15% of the college population have some symptoms of eating disorders; of those who have such symptoms, 87% are women. As a result of their observations of college women with eating disorders, authorities have recommended primarily three treatment approaches: affect-oriented support groups (Neuman & Halvorson, 1983), psychoeducational behavioral management treatment groups (Boskind-White & White, 1983), and insight-oriented individual therapy (Bruch, 1973; Neuman & Halvorson, 1983).

Two major assumptions underlie these recommendations. First, the primary

This author wishes to acknowledge the Director of the Springfield College Counseling Center, Dr. Richard A. Whiting's influence in providing the administrative leadership, clinical supervision and collegial support which allowed this work to happen.

55

focus of therapy should be on the individual. The goal is to help the woman gain control of her own behavior by sensitizing her to the affective and cognitive processes that surround the eating behavior and to those that are common to all women. The behaviors of the family and significant others are considered adjuncts with which the individual must learn to cope. Second, a group therapy format provides the most cost-effective treatment approach (Hornak, 1983; Loganbill, 1983) and an essential social support network (Boskind-White & White, 1983; Garner, Garfinkel, & Bemis, 1982; Neuman & Halvorson, 1983). Therefore, unless the client is insufficiently committed to change and disrupts the group process, a group treatment approach is recommended. Those who do not meet these criteria are referred for individual therapy. The relational patterns that support the eating disorder are viewed as outside the therapeutic milieu and are brought into the therapy only as causative factors.

These two assumptions have certain negative consequences for the treatment of bulimia and compulsive eating in the college setting, however. Conceptualizing the individual as the unit of treatment restricts the therapist's options for creating a viable therapeutic context, for example. In addition, models that are derived from this conceptualization do not adequately account for the uniqueness of the emergence and persistence of the eating disorder in each individual.

The systemic-theoretical base of family therapy has been applied to the treatment of eating disorders in a variety of public and private mental health care settings. This approach offers a considera-

tion of behavioral dimensions that are not considered in individual treatment models. In each of these family therapy models, behavior is perceived as interactional, and the unit of intervention is minimally the dyad or triad. These models include, either explicitly or implicitly, three dimensions of interactionality:

1. The developmental dimension. As opposed to viewing a problematic change in individual behavior as a response to personal physiological or social development, the systemic therapist views such a change as a message about difficulties of transition in the family's development (Haley, 1973; Minuchin, 1974).

2. The social context dimension. In order to understand the way in which behavior operates in a social context, it is necessary to define the therapeutic frame (i.e., the individuals and the interactional patterns that maintain the symptom). While systemic models focus primarily on families as the most significant social context, there is some evidence that problem-maintaining patterns can operate in nonfamilial systems (Imber-Black [Coppersmith], 1983; Selvini-Palazzoli, Boscolo, Cecchin, & Prata, 1980) and that the principles of systemic thinking can be applied with individuals or "parts of families" (Hoffman, 1981; Moley 1983; Weakland, 1983).

3. The symptom meaning dimension. The values, meanings, and beliefs that surround a symptom are unique to each social context. Systemic therapies emphasize the importance of learning the unique and personal

meaning that a behavior reflects in its particular context.

In the college counseling center, applications of a developmental interactional approach to the treatment of bulimia and compulsive eating (1) expand the treatment options of campus-based therapists when current models do not suffice and (2) suggest possibilities for adapting an interactional approach to treatment in an institution with constraints on the provision of its services.

THE SYMPTOM

Bulimia and compulsive eating are the two most common eating disorders in the college environment, and they are similar in their behavioral characteristics and interactional consequences. Both involve frequent episodes of the ingestion of massive quantities of food and are experienced as out of control of the individual. While bulimics go to great lengths to purge themselves of the food taken in and compulsive eaters retain the food, both groups find their lives organized around the preparations for eating, the struggle not to binge again, the increasing rejection of social encounters in favor of bingeing, and the maintenance of secrecy about their eating behavior. While their weight may fluctuate with short-term weight loss achieved by rigid dieting, the desired goal of permanent thinness is not achieved. This inability to maintain a consistent weight may be noticed by significant others, but the maintenance of a socially acceptable weight often differentiates bulimics and compulsive eaters from anorectics and obese individuals.

THE COLLEGE ENVIRONMENT

The treatment of eating disorders in a college counseling center takes place within an institution that has as its primary mission the provision of a voluntary educational opportunity for young adults. Because the provision of mental health services is secondary to the main function of the institution, the implicit goal in any therapy is to help the student succeed educationally, preferably on that particular campus. This goal is not problematic in itself, but the varied interpretations across campus of the appropriate way for the center to meet the goal requires different responses at different times. The administration of the center may be in the hands of individuals who are inexperienced in mental health services and inadvertently make policies that seriously limit the ability of therapists to work effectively. Some faculty members are highly supportive of therapy (more frequently referred to as "counseling"), viewing it as a solution to all problems; others are sharply critical, equating the services with those of a high school guidance office. The attitudes of other faculty members fall between these two extremes.

Mental health services are for the students, and most therapeutic encounters are initiated by students themselves. Implied in this arrangement is the allegiance of the therapist to the student, with the confidentiality of the therapist-client relationship held sacred. Thus, a therapist's request to bring in other family members may be viewed as a betrayal by the client. As a result, the young person may have more influence on the direction of therapy than the therapist deems appropriate.

College is almost by definition an opportunity for young adults to "try their wings" and experiment with independence from family guidance. Consequently, therapists at most college counseling centers assume that a student's problems should be resolved independent of family input in order to enhance the individuation process. Similarly, they frequently assume that they are not responsible for helping students with "serious" problems, seeing their function instead as the provision of crisis intervention or short-term support. If problems are not resolved within a few months, they refer students to community specialists or, at times, encourage them to go home.

The geographical distance between child and family, which may be a central piece of information in therapy, is a given of the college environment. In exercising their influence to develop a therapeutic context of the significant social system, therapists at college counseling centers must make concessions to this distance, particularly if the preferred treatment context includes the family. From the perspective of individual models of therapy, distance is a plus. From that of systemic therapies, it constrains the therapist's use of influence.

In many colleges, therapy is guided by the academic calendar. Even if the problem has not been resolved by June, therapy is terminated or at least postponed until September. The ebb and flow of predictable academic stresses during the year must be acknowledged, both in formulating a treatment plan and in evaluating the client's responses.

A DEVELOPMENTAL INTERACTIONAL APPROACH

An integration of the premises of developmental theory and the Brief Therapy Model of the Mental Research Institute provides a conceptual framework for the treatment of bulimia and compulsive eating.

Developmental Dimension

Bulimia and compulsive eating are most likely to become problems in middle to late adolescence, a time described as the "leaving home stage" of the family life cycle (Haley, 1980). The appearance of a symptom that inhibits the full pursuit of the activities of work, school, and relationships that are appropriate at this age can most easily be understood in relation to the dramatic changes required in all family relationships at this time. It is commonly assumed that only the young adult who leaves home for college is changing; in reality, the family is also changing as it adjusts to the lack of daily interaction between the student and each family member. Such a shift in the frequency and intensity of interaction may alter the established balance of complementarity and symmetry in relationships.

By definition, a developmental transition is one that requires new rules for the modulation of physical and psychological distance among the family members and between the family and other social contexts. Although bulimia and compulsive eating may appear "invisible," they regulate closeness and distance in social interaction. The sense of personal disgust and depression felt by bulimics and compulsive eaters triggers withdrawal from social encounters, often interfering with sexual involvements. In families with rules of relationship that proscribe further distance, eating disorders can simultaneously increase distance by creating a personal secret and maintain closeness by making it impossible for the student to pursue the college life fully. Sometimes, the disorder provides the rationale for infrequent visits home because the student does not want anyone to find out or for frequent visits home because the student feels too restricted in the dormitory.

Social Context Dimension

The basic premises of the Brief Therapy Model are that all behavior occurs in a social context and that behavior becomes patterned over time. Recurrent behavior can persist only if supported by the reciprocal responses of the members of the context (Watzlawick, Weakland, & Fisch, 1974; Weakland, 1983). The issue for the therapist is to identify the present sequence of behaviors that is maintaining the problem and the social context defined by that sequence of behaviors or "wrong solution cycle."

Every individual is part of a variety of social contexts simultaneously (e.g., the family, school, and work contexts). While it is generally accepted that the family is the social context with which the therapist should work (Haley, 1976; Minuchin, 1974; Selvini-Palazzoli, Boscolo, Cecchin, & Prata, 1980; Weakland, 1983), nonfamilial systems can also promote problem-maintaining "wrong solution cycles" (Imber-Black [Coppersmith], 1983; Selvini-Palazzoli, et al., 1980). Not all interactions within any given system, including the family, are relevant to the problem at hand.

. . . it makes much more sense to assume that some interactions, (and, equally, some relationships, since a relationship is mainly a summation or pattern of particular interactions) may be highly significant with respect to certain behaviors by certain persons, but of little relevance for other behaviors or persons. (Weakland, 1983, p. 3)

Although Weakland referred primarily to the family context in this passage, he did not exclude the applicability of the assumption to nonfamilial systems.

In the college setting, three social contexts have been found to be useful for organizing the treatment of bulimia and compulsive eating: (1) the family context, (2) the residential/friendship context, and (3) the individual context. In keeping with the Brief Therapy view, these contexts are merely invented realities (Watzlawick, 1984). They do not "exist" in isolation from each other and, in fact, influence each other as interactive contexts. Because they are not equally influential in all situations, it is not necessary to deal with all three in all cases.

Family Context

In the clinical literature based on systems theory, the greatest attention has been placed on the family context, defined in terms of the individuals and relational patterns that emerge from the identified patient's family of origin. Noticeable bulimic or compulsive eating behaviors or related changes in social behaviors in the college student may elicit the well-intentioned involvement of family members in the student's life, either through more frequent visits between parents and student or through more frequent telephone calls. Often, the student's secret is kept between one parent and the student, skewing relationships to a more rigid complementarity around parental functioning. For one parent, the distance between college and home decreases; for the other, it increases. From an interactional perspective, the bulimia or compulsive eating and related familial responses reflect the family's unsatisfactory accommodation to the developmental transition.

Residential/Friendship Context

In college, new social contexts are formed to facilitate the transition from home. The most significant systems, those with unique patterns of nurturance, problem solving, regulation of distance among members, and imposition of behavioral sanctions, often emerge from the residential environment. Given the proximity and intensity of their involvement in each other's lives, members of this support network commonly help each other in times of apparent need. The patterns that evolve may or may not be similar to those of the family contexts. The behaviors of the bulimic and compulsive eater, however triggered, are highly compelling in a context already sensitized to appearance, diet, and food in general.

Individual Context

Strictly speaking, individual behavior always has social consequences in that, either directly or indirectly, it elicits responses from others. Certain problems, however, can develop in a more private world, and a larger social context can become part of the problem-maintaining cycle even when no one is aware of the problem. When bulimia and compulsive eating episodes occur in secrecy,

as they often do, the solutions applied may be primarily a consequence of reciprocal feedback processes between the self's solution responses (Weakland, 1983). The therapist can direct treatment to this cycle, while bearing in mind its relationship to other social contexts.

Symptom Meaning Dimension

A number of authors have reflected on the meaning of food, eating, and attractiveness in the American culture and the relationship of these meanings to eating disorders (Harkaway, 1983; Moley, 1983; Orbach, 1978; Wooley & Wooley, 1980). Although these social meanings are highly significant, the fact remains that not all individuals develop eating disorders. Moreover, not all individuals who come from families that appear to place undue emphasis on eating-related topics develop eating disorders. It seems that eating disorders are associated with the combination of a certain contextual responsiveness to deviations from particular eating styles, plus a particular interactional solution applied at a particular time in the family life cycle.

An assessment of bulimic and compulsive eating behavior should include a critical conceptualization of the behavior's meaning. It is important to use the language of the client that reflects the meaning of the behavior to facilitate change (Watzlawick, Weakland, & Fisch, 1974; Weakland, 1983).

TREATMENT IN CONTEXT

The principles applied to the selection or creation of a viable therapeutic context in the treatment of eating disorders are the same as those applied in the treatment of other types of disorders. As Dammann and Berger suggested in illustrating the development of a therapeutic context with nonfamilial households, the therapist must "create a therapeutic unit which empowers a group of people who may not, prior to therapy, experience themselves as a therapeutic unit" (1983, p. 67). In the college setting, the therapist must consider a variety of situational and pragmatic factors.

The selection of the therapeutic context is based on an evaluation of the symptom in terms of four interactionally formulated questions:

1. How pervasive is the problem? The therapist must determine the problem's chronicity, acuteness, and intrusiveness into the lives of the identified patient and others. For example, have the episodes of bingeing and vomiting been of such frequency and duration that physiological side effects are apparent? Does vomiting occur in the student's dormitory room, interfering with the quality of living for a roommate?

2. To whom is the eating disorder the biggest problem? Has the problem been presented at the college counseling center by the student herself, by friends or roommates who are worried about or angered by the behavior, or by parents who are asking the center staff to act as local parents?

3. How accessible are the various parts of the significant system? Boyfriends at nearby colleges may be willing to participate in therapy, but parents who live out of state may refuse to attend therapy sessions.

4. What is the extent of the therapist's leverage with the identified signifi-

cant system? Is the identified patient adamant in refusing to include family members? Family members are usually included at the request of the therapist, which makes them invited guests or consultants to the therapist rather than voluntary clients. Gaining leverage with invited guests calls for maintaining a one-down position in relation to the family's contributions. Although Fisch, Weakland, and Segal (1982) have recommended taking a one-down position in relation to a client's behavior in general, maintaining this position with a self-defined client is quite different from maintaining it with other clients. The risk of having no leverage at all is much greater with clients who are not self-defined.

Family Contextual Treatment

The family should be developed as the therapeutic context (1) if the eating disorder becomes so acute that the student's physical well-being appears to be in danger and/or if multiple adjunctive symptoms, such as depression and poor academic performance, threaten the student's ability to remain on campus; (2) if the symptom existed for a year or more before the student left home; (3) if information obtained in individual interviews with the client reveals an escalating cycle of family involvement with the symptom; or (4) if the therapist has been working with the individual context for a period of time with no improvement and wants more information. The therapist may decide to construct a family therapy context after the first interview or not until several months later.

When the therapist has a relationship with the identified patient first, it may be necessary to address a few dimensions of the therapist-client relationship before moving to a family therapy context. Because of a belief that the center is primarily for students, some clients feel personally betrayed if the therapist asks to include the family in treatment. In order to prevent this sense of betrayal, the therapist can employ a variety of strategies to pave the way for the transition. For example, a therapist may contract with a student for a certain number of individual sessions with a stipulation that the therapist has the right to invite the family to sessions if the symptom does not improve. Frequently, it is useful to spend at least one meeting preparing for the new context by following a line of future questioning (Penn, 1985). Questions such as ''Who will be most upset to learn about your problem? If I were to ask the 'wrong question,' what would that be? Who would it be to? What is likely to happen between A and B if I ask that question?'' will help the client make the contextual transition.

At the end of the initial family session, the therapist may offer recommendations, ranging from contact at the family's discretion to periodic meetings of selected or all nuclear family members. Because of geographical restrictions, the most frequent arrangement with families is a contract for six sessions to be held at intervals of 2 to 4 weeks. In spite of the obvious inconvenience, parents have expressed pleasure at being included in therapy. As they have often been sitting at home feeling helpless to deal with their child's problem, they are very appreciative of the link between home and college.

Alana, a college junior, had been bulimic since her freshman year. She had been a little overweight in high school and, after she ended her relationship with her high school boyfriend, had started to binge and vomit so she would not gain weight. Alana was seen individually for approximately 6 months with no consistent reduction in the frequency of bingeing and vomiting, which took place on an average of five times each day. The therapist hypothesized that the family was the significant context when Alana explained her refusal to tell anyone in the family what was going on, particularly her mother, by saying that her mother had too many problems already, a not uncommon response of the bulimic. Alana presented herself as determined to conquer the problem by herself; therefore, the therapist described the proposal that Alana's family help her with this problem as merely a suggestion.

Alana's biological father had died when she was 3 years old. Her mother, Louise, had remarried when Alana was 8. There were two younger children by the second marriage, both of whom had problems; one was identified as learning disabled, and the other was "demanding and stubborn." Alana guarded the image of the family, reporting that the younger children were doing well now, and that she was very close to her mother. She also reported that she felt a little more uncomfortable with Steve, her stepfather; "he always told me I should lose a few pounds as a kid." Alana saw herself defined as the "good kid," the one who did not give the family any trouble. Being bulimic was being bad.

The therapist saw a more useful reality in the premise that, by being bad, Alana was being good. Her bulimic behavior appeared to modulate the distance between her and her stepfather; it inhibited her availability as a sexual partner (to her peers as well as to her stepfather) in a family that had not addressed sexual intimacy in nonbiological relations within a family. The bulimic behavior also allowed her to continue to be good by appearing good to her mother, who seemed genuinely oblivious to her situation.

The therapist decided that intervening through Alana with this reframing of her behavior would probably be less effective than intervening through Alana and her parents as a group. If Alana alone received such a message, it seemed likely that she would talk to her mother about it—if anyone—which might support the current skew of closeness and distance. If she kept the message to herself, she might continue to internalize all the responsibility for the problem and the solution.

The way was paved for including the family by introducing a line of hypothetical questioning about what might happen if Alana's mother and stepfather were at the session. The questions were intended to challenge the premises that supported an interactional conspiracy of silence about the bulimia, the implicit rule that "the best way to be good was to be bad," and the belief that acknowledgment of the problem would upset the balance of relationships in a way that might be dangerous for individuals or the family as a whole. After three preparatory sessions, Alana said she was afraid, but wanted to tell her mother the next time she went home. Her mother was responsive, indicating genuine surprise, and called the therapist to arrange to come to the counseling center with her husband. Interestingly, Alana's bingeing and purging decreased by half by the time the visit took place 2 weeks later.

As a consequence of the shift in Alana's behavior, the line of questioning during the interview with the parents focused on three themes. As consultants to the therapist, the parents were asked what their views were of Alana's struggles with weight and eating, who in the family was regarded as an expert on problems like this, and what their theories were about the nature of the problem. As guests, the parents were invited to ask the therapist questions about the therapy and the disorder itself. As parents, they were asked to decide if Alana should continue to resolve this problem alone or with the help of the family.

When Alana's mother asked the therapist what the prognosis was and why Alana was having this problem, the therapist offered the following explanation:

> It is my experience that one of the toughest things in stepfamilies is to figure out how close you can be without being too close and how distant you can be without being too distant. You think you've just got it figured out when one person changes and the whole balance is upset. Alana was trying not to upset the balance. She found a unique, though painful, way to keep the balance the same, even though she was

changing as an individual in a way that might change the closeness and distance between you. At this stage of life, when a daughter leaves home for college, she has become a young woman whose interest in intimate relationships outside the family frequently increases the distance between mother and daughter and develops a new closeness between father and daughter. In stepfamilies, this can be awkward. Alana's bulimia helped her to remain good as in her younger years—when she binged and vomited, it put a little distance between mother and daughter because she felt bad about having a secret from you, but appeared good because you didn't know. That kept the two of you as close as ever. Bingeing and vomiting was good for keeping distance between you, Steve, and Alana because the natural warmth, pride, and closeness you felt between you as she became a mature young woman was unfamiliar, but being bad made her stay a little girl who needed daddy. It would seem that it may no longer be necessary for Alana to be good by being bad, but it's too soon to tell.

Alana proceeded to talk to Steve about his proddings about her weight as a child. Steve admitted his own struggles with weight, and Louise acknowledged that she had never realized Steve's proddings were from protective concern. The family session provided an opportunity to interrupt the escalating cycle of pseudo-distancing between Alana and Steve and psuedo-closeness between Alana and Louise, and to begin to define their relationships through a more flexible complementarity.

Because the family members all agreed that Alana was getting better and she seemed to be doing it by herself, they decided family therapy was not necessary. They decided to return in a month to monitor Alana's progress. Alana continued to see the therapist individually. At the 1-month family follow-up, Alana was bingeing only once a week, and she had started to date for the first time in 18 months. Approximately 6 months after graduation, the therapist received a letter from Alana, stating that she was engaged and all was well.

Residential/Friendship Contextual Treatment

The non-familial context is rarely as powerful as is the family context in producing long histories of compulsive eating or bulimia. Under certain circumstances, however, the selection of the residential/friendship therapeutic context is appropriate. For example, the therapist may develop this context when the eating disorder symptoms are of relatively short duration, generally having begun after the student arrived on campus, and persist through the well-meant, but inappropriate solutions of a significant on-campus social context. Sometimes, one or more members of a friendship system seek help for one apparently symptomatic system member. At times, the client herself may report that her friends want to know how to help her.

These situations are not without complications. While accessibility of the therapeutic context is not a problem, therapeutic leverage is highly variable. Friends who seek assistance are often simultaneously experiencing worry about the problem and exasperation at the amount of their time that it is consuming. Their feelings of sympathy and protection alternate with feelings of criticism and rejection, and their expectations of therapy are not always clear. Furthermore, the development of maximal leverage with this system requires a routine acceptance of the friendship system's definition of the problem, which may differ from the identified patient's definition. In this event, the therapist runs the risk of alienating the potential client by sounding like an advocate for the group.

The goals of intervention and the time frame for therapy are best kept very limited when the residential/friendship therapeutic context is used. Sometimes, the goal is symptom alleviation; more often, it is to improve the relationships within the friendship system and to prepare the client to pursue other means to resolve the eating disorder symptoms.

In the following example, the therapist hypothesized that collusion in the denial of a problem by a friendship system comprised of a bulimic young woman and two friends was inhibiting therapeutic progress. The goal was to interrupt this collusion and "free up" the identified patient to be able to pursue a more productive response to her problem.

Andrea, a freshman, reported bingeing and vomiting approximately 12 times each week for several months. She laughed a great deal about the situation, was happy to have lost some weight through her eating style, and worried that she would get fat if she stopped this behavior. She appeared minimally concerned about the long-term ramifications. Initially, she expressed no other concerns and identified no one else as involved in her problem.

The therapist was cautious, saying that there was a solution to the prob-

lem, but that Andrea was not yet ready to take advantage of it. In the meantime, the therapist advised Andrea not to do anything different, except to keep track of her bulimic episodes to help the therapist learn more about the situation. Sessions continued for 1 month with some slight decrease in the frequency of episodes; but the constant levity indicated no real change, and tales of kidding among her friends about her behavior suggested the involvement of others in problem-maintaining behaviors. After missing one appointment, Andrea called for an urgent appointment. She appeared far more serious and concerned as she related a most humiliating experience. She was eating a sandwich with her freinds when "out of the blue" she vomited in front of them. Her interpretation of this event was that the situation was getting worse and more uncontrollable. The therapist soberly reframed her behavior: "Thank you for letting me and others know that it is time to take you more seriously." Andrea nodded and became tearful for the first time. She agreed to bring in the significant social network, which was composed of two friends, Carol and Maria.

When the threesome arrived, they displayed the same lightheartedness that Andrea had displayed in the initial individual sessions. Even in talking about the episode of vomiting that they had witnessed, their concern was hidden behind a style of comic understatement. It became clear, however, that Carol and Maria were engaged in a symmetrical escalation, pursuing very different styles of helping. Carol felt less influential as she tried to assume a more serious posture. She had discussed Andrea's problem with her own mother, who was sending her newspaper articles about eating disorders. Carol would try to prevent Andrea from overeating in the cafeteria, saying to her, "I'm extra hungry tonight. Can I eat your dessert?" Maria would support the joking, but would try to cajole Andrea out of eating certain foods and would also eat food from her plate. She would organize late evening social events to get Andrea out of her room and away from food. Andrea appeared to prefer Maria's solution, but defeated both.

The most stressful moment in the interview occurred when the therapist asked Andrea if this helping helped. She quietly said, "No," and indicated that Carol and Maria did not know how she felt—which she quickly disconfirmed by making a joke. The therapist decided to interrupt this escalating cycle of pseudo-solutions and the complementarity reflected in the one-up position of the joined Maria and Andrea in relation to the one-down position of Carol. The task was an application of the "pretend technique" (Madanes, 1981), which capitalized on the system's playfulness. Because this interview had been identified as a consultation, the therapist offered the task as a suggestion. Learning that neither Carol nor Maria knew how frequently the bulimic episodes occurred, the therapist suggested that they try to figure out how many times a week Andrea was actually bingeing and vomiting. Andrea was still not to change the frequency of her bulimic episodes, but she was to report some episodes to both girls as soon after as possible, not to report others, and to report having had episodes a few times when she had not. Carol and Maria were to see if they could distinguish which episodes were real. The therapist vaguely suggested that this might help them decide how best to help, and they could all come back and let her know what they learned the following week—if they thought the information would help the therapist. The invitation was left open, because the therapist was unconvinced of the friendship system's comfort with the involvement in the therapy.

The day before the next scheduled appointment, Andrea called to say that Maria was leaving early for vacation and that she herself had a great deal of work to do, but she was feeling better. She rescheduled an appointment for all three the week after vacation, but only Andrea came. She confessed that they had not done the task. She had "reported in" a couple of times, but she did not want to and her friends did not seem to want to hear. The last 2 weeks had been better in terms of the frequency of bingeing and vomiting, but her mother had "found out" when she was home and wanted her to see a therapist at home. She said that was OK with her, because it might be helpful just to "get away from campus with the problem." She thought her friends were more relaxed, knowing that her mother knew. The long-term outcome of this case is not known.

Individual Contextual Treatment

The major portion of clinical work at a college counseling center, regardless of the problem, is with individuals; however, the premises of systems-based models guide treatment. For example, the conceptualization of behavior from an interactional perspective is in the mind of the therapist, not in the number of people in the therapy room; change in one individual ripples throughout the system; and working with the most stressed individual in the system increases the chances of resolving the problem. Thus, the therapeutic context is defined as the individual (1) when the student requests therapy and appears to be the most stressed by the identified problem, and (2) when other members of the identified significant system are not accessible, either because of geographical distance or because of personal withdrawal.

The fact that bulimia and compulsive eating often remain totally hidden from significant others makes it easier for the therapist to look at the problem as one maintained by self-to-self systemic processes. Nevertheless, there are certain special considerations in working with individuals on a college campus from an interactional perspective. Respect for the confidentiality of the therapist-client relationship must be mutually affirmed. Although the nature of interventions should always be consistent with that of the larger context, strategic interventions that have emerged from systemic therapies can appear bizarre when extracted from the therapeutic context. If students share the happenings of therapy with friends, the impact of interventions may be reduced, or the negative judg-

ments of other students about the nature of the help may be increased. Similarly, therapists at college counseling centers should not ask students to perform tasks that will bring any more critical attention to them than already exists.

Susan, a college sophomore, had gained 25 pounds since she came to college. She indicated that she had always struggled to lose 10 pounds and maintain the loss in high school, but that she had never weighed so much. She had tried a variety of diets and had read many articles on the psychological aspects of eating, diets, and nutrition (as have most individuals absorbed in the weight gain-weight loss syndrome). This was her first experience with therapy, and while she called it "her last hope," it seemed to the therapist that she was quite uncomfortable with the idea and would not give the therapist much time to work with her. This may have been in part a consequence of a strong orthodox religious background that encouraged problem resolution through faith rather than through secular means. The therapist conceptualized a solution cycle of vowing to start a diet tomorrow and not being able to sustain a diet, behavior that triggered self-deprecating thoughts. When she felt desperate, she would confess her bingeing and diet violations to God and "bargain" with God to give her strength in handling this problem.

The cycle is typical of the compulsive eater's responses—with the unique invocation of God's support. To interrupt this cycle, the therapist took the position that Susan was right, that therapy was not the best way to solve this problem. Successful dieting is like a religious experience, offered the therapist, and is a matter of having faith. The best that the therapist could offer was to meet for 5 weeks to determine whether Susan had faith. If she agreed to this, she would be asked to do a variety of homework tasks that would indicate her level of faith and, therefore, her readiness to lose weight. The tasks would require complete honesty, but only Susan would know if she were honest, because faith is an inner experience. Susan agreed to the contract, and the tasks included recording everything she ate, reporting her actual weight to the therapist, outlining the consequences of change, and going to church to confess more directly to God. At the end of the 5 weeks, Susan had lost 8 pounds. Therapy was terminated with the suggestion that Susan let the therapist know what was happening—if she wanted to do so. Susan came by at the end of the year, approximately 3 months later, having lost another 10 pounds.

An analysis of this case from an interactional perspective reveals that the solution cycle was interrupted by applying Susan's reality of the importance of faith to the problem-maintaining solution of planned dieting. Instead of expending her energies to diet, she was directed to assess her readiness to diet by examining her level of faith. There has been no long-term follow-up of this case.

CONCLUSION

The developmental interactional perspective that has been applied to the treatment of eating disorders can be generalized to other problems that arise for treatment in a college counseling center, such as academic failure, depression, psychotic episodes, phobic behaviors, social incompetence, and disability adjustment (Whiting, Terry, & Strom-Henricksen, 1984). This model does not replace other models of therapy, however, nor is it a panacea for "curing" symptoms that have resisted "cure" when treated through other models. It is guided by the same premise that underlies the systemic paradigm in general—it increases therapeutic options for helping individuals resolve problems.

The present evolutionary stage of this model leaves a number of areas open for development. For example, it is necessary to assess the limits of working without the family context, particularly when the client is not highly motivated. Counseling center therapists, together with other on-campus helpers, need to develop a process of generating concern in the client when the client and the family are colluding to deny the existence of a problem. In addition, the decision not to work with a family is frequently based on logistical issues rather than on theoretical formulations. Nevertheless, our center's work has been enhanced and the success rate increased by the applications of an interactional approach. Furthermore, the values promoted by the staff have begun to make inroads at administrative levels regarding the traditional assumptions made about the student's development at the leaving home stage of the family life cycle.

REFERENCES

Boskind-Ledahl, M., & White, W.C. (1978). The definition and treatment of bulimarexia in college women—A pilot study. *Journal of the American College Health Association, 27,* 84–86.

Boskind-White, M., & White, W.C. (1983). *Bulimarexia: The binge/purge cycle.* New York: W.W. Norton.

Bruch, H. (1973). *Eating disorders: Obesity, anorexia and the person within.* New York: Basic Books.

Dammann, C., & Berger, M. (1983). Household and family—Creating a workable treatment unit. *Journal of Strategic and Systemic Therapies, 2,* 67–73.

Fisch, R., Weakland, J., & Segal, L. (1982). *Tactics of change.* San Francisco: Jossey-Bass.

Garner, D.M., Garfinkel, P.E., & Bemis, K.M. (1982). A multidimensional psychotherapy for anorexia nervosa. *International Journal of Eating Disorders, 1,* 3–46.

Haley, J. (1973). *Uncommon therapy.* New York: W.W. Norton.

Haley, J. (1976). *Problem-solving therapy.* San Francisco: Jossey-Bass.

Haley, J. (1980). *Leaving home.* New York: McGraw-Hill.

Halmi, K.A., Falk, J.R., & Schwartz, E. (1981). Binge-eating and vomiting: A survey of a college population. *Psychological Medicine, 11,* 697–706.

Harkaway, J. (1983). Obesity: Reducing the larger system. *Journal of Strategic and Systemic Therapies, 2,* 2–14.

Hoffman, L. (1981). *Foundations of family therapy.* New York: Basic Books.

Hornak, N.J. (1983). Group treatment for bulimia: Bulimics anonymous. *Journal of College Student Personnel, 24,* 461–462.

Imber-Black (Coppersmith), E. (1983). The place of family therapy in the homeostasis of larger systems. In M. Aronson & R. Wolberg (Eds.), *Group and family therapy.* New York: Brunner/Mazel.

Katzman, M., & Wolchik, S. (1984). Bulimia and binge eating in college women: A comparison of personality and behavioral characteristics. *Journal of Consulting and Clinical Psychology, 52,* 423–428.

Loganbill, C. (1983). Eating disorder group. *Journal of College Student Personnel, 24,* 274–275.

Madanes, C. (1981). *Strategic family therapy.* San Francisco: Jossey-Bass.

Minuchin, S. (1974). *Families and family therapy.* Cambridge, MA: Harvard University Press.

Minuchin, S., Rosman, B., & Baker, L. (1978). *Psychosomatic families: Anorexia Nervosa in context.* Cambridge, MA: Harvard University Press.

Moley, V. (1983). The interactional treatment of eating disorders. *Journal of Strategic and Systemic Therapies, 2,* 10–28.

Neuman, P., & Halvorson, P. (1983). *Anorexia nervosa and bulimia.* New York: Van Nostrand Reinhold.

Orbach, S. (1978). *Fat is a feminist issue.* New York: Berkeley.

Penn, P. (1985). Feed-forward: Future questioning, future maps. *Family Process, 24,* 299–310.

Selvini-Palazzoli, M. (1974). *Self-starvation.* London: Chaucer.

Selvini-Palazzoli, M., Boscolo, L., Cecchin, G., & Prata, G. (1978). *Paradox and counterparadox.* New York: Jason Aronson.

Selvini-Palazzoli, M., Boscolo, L., Cecchin, G., & Prata, G. (1980). The problem of the referring person. *Journal of Marital and Family Therapy, 6,* 3–9.

Watzlawick, P. (1984). *The invented reality.* New York: W.W. Norton.

Watzlawick, P., Weakland, J., & Fisch, R. (1974). *Change.* New York: W.W. Norton.

Weakland, J. (1983). Family therapy with individuals. *Journal of Strategic and Systemic Therapies, 2,* 1–9.

Weinstein, H., & Richman, A. (1984). The group treatment of bulimia. *Journal of American College Health, 32,* 208–215.

Whiting, R., Terry, L., & Strom-Henricksen, H. (1984). From home to college, from college to home: An interactional approach to treating symptomatic disabled college students. In E. Imber-Black (Coppersmith) (Ed.), *Families with handicapped members,* (pp. 30–43). Rockville, MD: Aspen Publishers.

Wooley, S.C., & Wooley, O.W. (1980). Eating disorders: Obesity and anorexia. In A. Brodsky & R. Hare-Mustin (Eds.), *Women and psychotherapy.* New York: Guilford Press.

6

Family Fat: Assessing and Treating Obesity within a Family Context

Joseph H. McVoy, Jr., PhD
Director
Department of Family Therapy
Saint Albans Psychiatric Hospital
Radford, Virginia

THERE MAY BE NO GREATER preoccupation in the United States than the concern of its citizens over their body weight. This obsessive concern is reflected in the millions of dollars spent annually on diet books, diet foods, diet centers, and "weight loss" therapy. This cultural hysteria over thinness is fueled by the real issues of the health risk and societal stigmatization associated with obesity.

Society's obsessiveness about weight and the serious psychological and biological sequelae of obesity have generated extensive research in the fields of genetics, endocrinology, nutrition, pharmacology, psychology, and sociology (Powers, 1980). This has led to an enormous accumulation of knowledge about obesity, but, paradoxically, little or no progress in its amelioration. Reviewers of treatment outcome literature continue to assert that no treatment approach has yet produced appreciable long-term results (Stalanos, 1985; Stunkard, 1980).

Recent attempts to cut this Gordian knot have moved away from the microworld of the fat cell to the macroworld of the obese person in his or her total context. The fat cell then becomes merely the repository of the multifarious issues of family history and environment. In this view, although the family exists in a context of community and societal factors, the family itself is the keystone to an understanding and treatment of obesity.

The importance of family was first prophetically described by Bruch and Touraine (1940) in a study of families with obese children. They found that the mothers of these children were dominating and excessively protective, while the fathers were less involved and nonaggressive. These characteristics, as Bruch and Touraine described them, are similar to those of the psychosomatic family, as first described by Minuchin, Rosman, and Baker (1978). Although one recent research study (Vandereycken, 1986) failed to support the model of Minuchin and his colleagues, other researchers have presented evidence that aspects of psychosomatic families can be found among the families of the obese (Ganly, 1985; Harkaway, 1986; Wiley, 1979). Another has proposed that these characteristics are found only in a specific subpopulation of families (McVoy, 1980).

Although family dynamics have been recognized as an important contributing factor in obesity, little has been done to develop an effective treatment approach that is based on family therapy. Most reports of family involvement have come not from family therapists, but from behaviorally oriented therapists (LeBow, 1984). Harkaway (1983), however, has attempted to adapt specific family therapy techniques to the treatment of obesity. She has offered therapeutic solutions that, although they do not constitute a discrete treatment model, provide an important bridge between conventional obesity treatment and family therapy.

Any effective treatment strategy for obesity must include provisions both for the weight loss itself and for any necessary changes in the family dynamics, because current research indicates that most dieting behavior is counterproductive to weight loss (Polivy & Herman, 1983). Moreover, trying to lose weight without physical exercise is also not productive. Stunkard (1984) noted that physical activity is essential. Consequently, a well-developed obesity treatment program must integrate treatment of family dynamics as a causal factor of obesity with other aspects, including physiological, environmental, emotional, and cognitive factors. Without such an approach, the therapist may experience a frustrating pattern of partial success. For example, success is limited if treatment resolves family issues that contribute to an adolescent's severe obesity, but does not help the family accomplish the difficult task of weight loss. Similarly, unless therapy that helps an obese homemaker to resolve the emotional issues related to binge eating and to lose weight also deals with the systemic changes that will result from her weight loss, the homemaker is likely to regain that weight.

The very complexity of the obesity system suggests that its treatment cannot be reduced to one universal approach. In fact, there is not one obesity, but many "obesities" (Young, 1964). They share the biological consequences of weight gain (i.e., the body state), but they have many different causes. Obesity may occur in association with a psychosomatic family, it may be the symptom of a marital hierarchical incongruity (Madanes, 1981), or it may result from the unfortunate combination of environmental factors and extreme biological vulnerability. For example, the obesity of a 280-pound woman who suddenly and rapidly gained weight at marriage is likely to differ both biologically and systemically from the obesity of a 280-pound woman who has been very obese since early childhood. Consequently, a thorough assessment is a critical first step in any treatment.

ASSESSMENT

Several theoretical assumptions form the foundation for obesity assessment:

1. There is for each individual an inherited biological predisposition toward obesity or leanness. This predisposition can be an important factor in the initiation and maintenance of obesity.
2. The age of onset is an important factor in obesity. There are marked differences between childhood onset obesity and adult onset obesity, with childhood onset obesity more resistant to treatment.
3. Marital and family stress can be an important causal or perpetuating factor for obesity. Eating may be a response to the perceived emotional stress.
4. Attempts to ameliorate the obesity are often major factors in its continuation and exacerbation, because they may lead to overinvolvement of family members or the use of rigid fasting diets that biologically perpetuate the obesity.
5. At times, obesity is tied to a three-generational transmission process similar to the multigenerational transmission process of Bowen (Hall, 1983). If, for example, the grandmother had an enmeshed relationship with the mother and conveyed significant anxiety about weight issues to her, the mother may develop an equally enmeshed relationship with her own daughter and, in her anxiety, pursue the daughter about being thin to the point that the daughter gains weight.

In order to unravel the interactions that have led to the obesity, assessment must tap all areas of information:

- the obese person's weight and nutritional history
- dieting attempts
- historical events in the family
- family interactions around weight and eating
- a family obesity history for at least three generations
- the presence of binge eating and bulimic behavior

Much of this information can be obtained by having the family complete a standardized obesity history inventory, such as the Stanford Eating Disorder Clinic Questionnaire (Powers, 1980). A family assessment session is important to observe the family interactional process. Structural therapy techniques for mapping the family (Minuchin et al., 1978), circular questioning (Penn, 1982), and the evaluation of the various solutions used to help the obese person (Fisch, Weakland, & Segal, 1982) are all useful information-gathering tools. Because such a plethora of specific information is necessary, a semistructured interview format can be helpful.

In addition, it is very helpful to obtain a family obesity genogram in order to place the obesity in the context of the family's transgenerational process. The therapist gathers information to complete a three-generational genogram (Bowen, 1978), giving particular attention to the body weights of family members and to their attitudes about obesity. It is also helpful to determine the emotional values placed on eating and the actual process of eating meals within the family. Such a genogram may reveal the transmission of obesity within a family, whether from genetic or environmental factors, and the influence of the family members' view about obesity on their response to the obese person.

A 40-year-old morbidly obese woman who had been overweight "all of my life" was found to have been "predestined" for obesity before birth. Her mother's family, all of whom were fair-skinned and thin, hated her father's family, all of whom were dark-haired, "hairy," and fat. The mother had worried incessantly during her pregnancy that her child would be born "one of them." The daughter was, in fact, born with a full head of black hair, and this prophecy, which she knew of as a child, was a fountainhead for her own personal sense of shame, isolation, and continued weight gain.

In another family, there was no obesity in the family history to explain why the client, a 35-year-old woman, had begun a sudden and steady increase in weight during the third grade. The genogram revealed that her father's family had a long history of alcoholism and that her father had begun drinking actively at the time of her initial weight gain. Not only did the father cause turmoil in the family by his abusive behavior and drinking, but also the mother was emotionally withdrawn.

This was a family where everyone seemed to live in a different house. The family members seldom ate meals together and had no recollection of any ritualistic family meals, such as Thanksgiving or Christmas dinners. In fact, the only signs of affection in this family were a pot of, as the client described it, "something

always on the stove" and the presence of plenty of cakes and pies in the kitchen. So the daughter ate constantly and gained weight. Also, it was revealed that the mother focused her energy on the daughter's obesity, which took center stage and allowed both mother and daughter to avoid dealing with the father's alcoholism.

In evaluating the assessment information, the therapist must consider the degree of obesity. Pragmatically, it is more difficult and takes longer to treat a client who weighs more than 400 pounds than to treat one who weighs 150 pounds. Not only do the very obese have secondary medical complications, but also they must make a greater long-term commitment to lose such a massive amount of weight. Furthermore, the more obese the person, the greater the changes in his or her appearance with weight loss. This increases the possibility that a family member will react negatively to the weight loss and become a saboteur of success (Marshall & Neill, 1977). Although it is not essential to have a formal diagnostic criteria for weight, it is useful to distinguish those who are moderately overweight (i.e., 20% to 50% over recommended body weight) from those who are severely overweight (i.e., 50% to 100% over recommended body weight). Both groups are potentially different from those who are morbidly obese (i.e., more than 100% in excess of recommended body weight).

The age of onset of the obesity can be an important clue in determining the likely degree of genetic and environmental involvement. It can also suggest the extent to which the person has inculcated a "fat" self-image that may develop a life of its own outside family dynamics. Those who have "always" been obese must deal not only with issues of family dynamics that have led to the obesity, but also with issues of self-perception. These people have no index for change, having always been perceived as obese; often, influenced by family and societal stigmatization, they feel inherently inferior and defective (Kaufman, 1980).

Equally important are the age of treatment and its difference from the age of onset. The treatment of a 12-year-old obese child is substantially different from the treatment of a 16-year-old adolescent or that of a 40-year-old adult. Moreover, if the adult who seeks treatment has been obese since early childhood, he or she is likely to present a different obesity system than is a similar-aged adult who became obese after marriage.

The information gathered in assessment can be used to make some early suppositions for the initial stages of therapy. When a parent brings a child for treatment of obesity, for example, usually the greater the disparity between the degree of obesity and the degree of parental concern, the greater the likelihood that the "obesity" is a symptom of other family stresses. This is particularly true when the child who is presented for treatment is only marginally overweight, but the parent is very invested in helping the child. It is important in these cases for the therapist to accept the family view that the weight is a problem, even though the therapist is aware that weight reduction will not be the primary goal of therapy. By accepting the family's perception of the "problem," the therapist makes it possible to deal with the problem for which the "obesity" is a metaphor.

TREATMENT

There are three distinct developmental periods in a client's life that dictate a different form of treatment: (1) prepubertal childhood, (2) adolescence, and (3) adulthood.

Prepubertal Childhood

When treating a prepubertal child for obesity, the therapist must focus primarily on the parents. It is usually the parents' concern, not the child's, that has led to treatment. Yet, paradoxically, it is the parents who can control changes in food intake and environment so that the child loses weight. The therapist should determine early in the assessment process why the parents have not made such changes. It is, therefore, very important to examine the family structure to learn just where the obesity of the child fits within the family system.

It is also important to find out what the parents have already tried to help the child lose weight. Often, they have threatened and cajoled, but have not structured the child's eating patterns. Parents have great anxiety about "starving" their child. If the parents' attempted solutions have been ineffectual, the therapist may begin treatment by structuring a solution in which the parents control food access and actively encourage the child to be more physically active. The type of physical activity, whether with the parents or away from the parents, is best determined by the degree of enmeshment and overprotectiveness of the parents.

If there are other family issues tied to the weight concerns, agent provocateurs will quickly appear. A parent, a sibling, or, often, a grandparent may be such an agent. It is not unusual to find that a child whose food intake is being restricted by his or her parents is being covertly fed by a grandparent. When this occurs, the real issue is often that the parent has not yet differentiated from his or her own parent; the child's eating becomes their symbolic tie. In this case, the therapist should involve all generations of the family in the treatment process.

The parents seek very specific advice and usually want the therapist to prescribe a diet for their child. It can be useful to refer them to a nutritionist who can provide them with the "diet" information they desire, but it is important to consider the negative effects of placing the child on a diet. Such a "solution" labels the child as a problem and establishes a pattern of dieting that has been shown to perpetuate weight gain rather than weight loss (Polivy & Herman, 1983). It is preferable to teach the parents to manage the child's intake in a less structured manner. If they first replace the junk food snacks that the child enjoys with low-calorie snacks and then change the family diet to a more healthy one, weight loss is often adequate. If not, the parents can gradually reduce the quantity of food that the child eats until a reasonable weight loss begins. It is important in all of these cases, particularly with children, that the therapist confer with the family physician concerning dietary plans.

As they gain weight, many children seem to reduce their physical activity, which, of course, leads to more weight gain and less physical activity. The rea-

son may be as simple as the child spends more and more time watching TV, or as complex as the child stays with the mother in response to the mother's needs. One study has shown that family environmental changes, such as moves to different geographical areas can set off a process of decreased physical activity that leads to major weight gain (Rona & Chinn, 1982). Whatever the reason, it is essential to change that cycle. Again, it is best to avoid formal exercise programs that may label the child and, instead, to involve the child in more normal and socially reinforcing activities, such as school events, recreational park events, or family activities.

Seeing these obese children only with their parents, therapists can use a number of differing family therapy approaches. Structural family therapy can be quite effective, especially when it is necessary to involve a disengaged father or to disengage an enmeshed, overprotective mother. Involving the child in more physical activities and using the disengaged parent as the "coach" make up one such approach.

Strategic therapy is quite useful in blocking behaviors that continue even after their results have been labeled ineffective or negative.

One mother literally hovered around her child at dinner, encouraging the child to eat less while at the same time putting large portions of food on the plate. The mother continued to do this, even after its negative effects were explained to her. Therefore, she was told that it would be more helpful if she would carry this behavior merely one step further. She was instructed to fix the child's plate, take what she thought was an excessive amount of food off the plate, and add it to hers. Because the mother was very concerned about gaining weight herself, she elected to serve her child smaller portions and to be silent about what the child ate.

The brief therapy techniques developed at the Mental Research Institute are also useful, especially when the parents refuse to stop trying their ''solutions'' (Fisch, Weakland, & Segal, 1982).

One mother who would not relent in maintaining a strict calorie count of everything the child ate was asked to keep more exact logs not only of all caloric intake and the specific time of that intake, but also of all physical activity so that she could calculate and adjust either the activity or intake as needed. After a day of this, she elected to try the method recommended by the therapist.

Quite often, parental enmeshment with the child or detoured marital conflict is the overriding factor in the treatment of prepubertal childhood obesity. Until these dysfunctional family dynamics are in some degree improved, it is often difficult to make progress in dealing with the weight issues. At such times, it is appropriate to see the parents separately to deal with other issues. The therapist must be sure to obtain permission from the parents before proceeding into this area, however.

Adolescence

Obese adolescents present a different and more complex dynamic than the younger child does. Those who were obese in early childhood have entered their adolescence identified as a fat kid. The therapist must deal with the precipitating factors that led to their obesity many years earlier, probably a history of inappropriate solutions, and often an internalized sense of being personally defective.

Those who became obese in adolescence do not have that long-term image of themselves as a fat kid. They often have a heightened sense that they are out of control, however, because their obesity has developed at a time when they are more focused on their body image. This group is often at risk of anorexia nervosa or bulimia. They are also more likely to have current family issues associated with their obesity.

Adolescents eat in more varied settings and for more varied reasons. Dieting becomes meaningful to adolescents as a social ritual, and looking good becomes a critical, conscious goal. Consequently, adolescents are more actively involved in creating their own maladaptive solutions for obesity, solutions that are independent of parental input.

Family interactions continue to be very important. In a family crisis, the adolescent may use eating to help solve the problem or release the tension.

One severely obese adolescent boy literally took to his bed and had his mother bring food to him all day long. It was clear later that his behavior was tied to a realization of his mother's deep depression, which led to her suicide during this period. Following her death, the son underwent therapy and was able to control his eating behaviors.

Often, parents suddenly realize that the ''baby fat'' is not going to disappear, and they become fanatical in their attempts to turn their ugly duckling into a beautiful adolescent swan. This can intensify and perpetuate the problem. Finally, eating can be a powerful act of rebellion for the adolescent. Minuchin and his colleagues (1978) pointed this out in their studies of anorectic adolescents, and the same dynamic can be seen with the bingeing teen-ager. Again, thorough assessment is critical.

When the obese adolescent's parents are overly involved in the dietary process, structural and strategic techniques may be used to block them, just as they are used to block the obese child's parents.

A morbidly obese adolescent girl continued to eat both secretively and publicly, despite her mother's daily barrage of comments that she was overweight and her clothes did not fit her. These comments led to protracted arguments between mother and daughter that left the daughter very depressed. When depressed, the daughter binged, setting the stage for a repetition of this scenario. Because the mother did not respond to a direct explanation of this, the daughter was told to carry a bag of Hershey kisses in her purse and to eat one kiss silently each time her mother commented on her weight. Within a week, the mother returned the bag of kisses, announcing that she did not need these anymore. The daughter began losing weight as she gradually withdrew from her intense relationship with her mother.

When emotional or rebellious issues are involved, they must be dealt with in a family therapy context. Again, dealing with these issues does not ensure that the teen-ager will lose weight. Helping the adolescent to lose weight requires a different approach.

Because the obese adolescent often has an enmeshed parent and quite often has an overprotective parent as well, it may be helpful to remove the weight loss process from the family. Until therapy, the adolescent's weight has been the focus and the property of the family system. In many cases, mothers of obese adolescents have been actively involved for years, helping them with diets and even dieting with their children. Taking the treatment of the obesity out of the family symbolically tells the family that the adolescent's body is his or her own responsibility. Of course, the therapist must keep the parents involved in other areas so that they do not sabotage the therapy. The mother may be asked to work separately with the nutritionist in meal planning, for example. The family should also be involved in periodic family therapy sessions to process and restructure interactional patterns that are negatively affecting the family.

A treatment group of six to eight adolescents replaces the family. This group begins with a focus on the presented problem, obesity, by providing information on the reasons that most diets do not work, setpoint theory, environmental and cognitive roadblocks, and emotionally triggered eating patterns. The sessions are oriented to problem solving and involve tasks to be performed between sessions.

The group is not truly weight-oriented in that there are no rigid weight loss goals; such overfocusing on the scale can be a disastrous "solution." Instead, assisted by a nutritionist, these adolescents learn to lose weight without the rigid structure of most diets. As group cohesiveness develops, family and individual issues are discussed. Each adolescent's genogram is presented, and family patterns that relate to eating are examined. The group members develop "hypotheses" about the ways in which they or their families will sabotage success and suggest tasks to use in blocking the saboteurs.

Many of these adolescents, especially those who have been obese since childhood, exhibit characteristics associated with co-dependency (Subby & Friel, 1984):

1. difficulty in expressing feelings
2. difficulty in maintaining close relationships
3. difficulty in making decisions or adjusting to change
4. an excessive sense of responsibility for others' behaviors and feelings
5. a constant need for others' approval to feel good
6. a sense of powerlessness in controlling their life
7. a self-image of themselves as inherently defective, a basic sense of shame, and low self-esteem

The group is an effective modality for helping adolescents overcome their sense of "defectiveness." Changes in personal appearance are encouraged, and the group members often help each other with shopping and, for the adolescent girl, makeup.

Many of these adolescents, especially those who have been obese since early childhood, have had very little regular physical activity. Therefore, the group is also involved three times each week in a physical activity program that includes walking, resistant exercises, and aerobics to improve their physical endurance and strength. Not only does this aid in long-term success, but also they see these improvements very quickly. This provides motivation in the early stages before they see significant weight loss.

Because many adolescents have dysfunctional cognitive beliefs that hinder progress, group members are taught cognitive-behavioral techniques to challenge their own thoughts and behaviors. All this, of course, promotes appropriate individuation. Their success is often a problem for others in the family. Consequently, family therapy sessions are essential to integrate the changes.

Adulthood

Obesity in the adult has an even wider spectrum than does obesity in the child or adolescent. At one extreme is the morbidly obese adult who has been obese since early childhood and has been on a roller coaster of weight gain and loss for years. At the other extreme is the adult who has suddenly gained weight after a specific event or developmental transition in life. Furthermore, there is a higher proportion of severe obesity among adults than among children or adolescents. Whereas the child and the adolescent are part of an existent family structure, this is not always the case for the adult. Thus, the adult may have no family available to be involved in the treatment process. Of those who do, there are usually significant issues of ongoing enmeshment in the family of origin or of the obesity's effect on the obese person's marriage.

Treatment of the adult marks a further shift in the treatment emphasis toward a group modality. In the group treatment of adult women and men, however, it is important to recognize the differences in their obesity. If the group process is to be truly effective, the moderately obese should be in a separate group from the severely and morbidly obese. Their issues are different, and their treatments follow different courses. Particularly for the very overweight, the group provides an acceptance and a sense of commonality that they may never have experienced in the past.

The spouse should be involved in couple sessions, particularly if weight has been a battleground for the couple. Spouses have often sent their partner to "get fixed" in various weight programs, and then they habitually complain about their partner's failure to lose weight. Because the spouses are not used to being involved themselves, engaging them can serve several purposes. It helps the assessment process, frequently blocks the tendency of a spouse to sabotage the process, and makes it possible to ease into marital therapy, which is often needed. Also, ongoing marital therapy can help reduce the stress that changes associated with weight loss may cause. Where possible, significant members of the family of origin should be included. The degree of their involvement should be dictated by the influence that they currently exercise over the obese person.

This treatment follows a pattern similar to that of the adolescent group. Many of the same issues are addressed, and the exercise group is the essential part of the program.

Treatment Team

Clearly, the use of a treatment team that includes a nutritionist and a physical activity specialist to assist the therapist facilitates the treatment of obesity. This may seem impractical, if not impossible, to a privately practicing clinician. In pragmatic terms, however, it is not as difficult as it first appears.

Nutritionists who are willing to work on an hour-to-hour consulting basis are available in most communities. By canvassing the local area, it is easy to find a qualified nutritionist to support the goals of therapy. In order to find a physical activity specialist and a physical plant for this part of the program, it is necessary only to investigate the local gyms and fitness centers. Hospital-affiliated fitness centers are ideal, because they can assume responsibility for any medical complications. The physical activity leader must be, or have available, a qualified physical therapist. The obese often have physical problems that could be exacerbated by improper activity, and an untrained aerobics instructor lacks the necessary knowledge of physiology to lead such a group safely.

This approach is more extensive than is that used by most therapists. Yet, to do less can be equated to seeing a client individually when it is clear that family issues are unresolved.

CASE STUDY

The following case study is atypical. The obesity of this adolescent was much more severe than that usually seen, and he was initially treated in an inpatient program. This case graphically illustrates the issues discussed, however.

Johnny, aged 18, had lived all his life in a rural Appalachian community. He was referred for treatment because of his morbid obesity; when first seen, he weighed 540 pounds. He was 6 feet tall and in remarkably good health, considering his weight. His primary physical difficulty was respiratory—he would be out of breath after walking as little as 20 yards. His father was a normal weight construction worker, and his mother was a normal weight home-maker. His 24-year-old brother, who had been out of the home for 4 years, was also of normal weight. Johnny had two aunts who were severely obese, but there appeared to be no consistent pattern of obesity in his family.

He was labeled a "fat" kid in the second grade. His parents' attempts to control his weight were unsuccessful, and his weight continued to climb. By age 13, he weighed 320 pounds. At that time, the family physician recommended that Johnny undergo jejunoileal bypass operation, which was performed that year. He had a small initial weight loss, but soon began methodically to regain the weight. Johnny had found that he could overcome the limiting effects of the bypass by, as he called it, "chipping." All day, he would eat small amounts of potato chips, washing them down with Coke.

The parents had a long history of marital conflict. The father worked 12 to 16 hours a day and was not involved in the family at all. This had led to a parental divorce several years earlier. The parents had since remarried, but they were, in effect, living separate lives.

During Johnny's childhood and adolescence, his father's parents were overly involved with both Johnny and the family. In fact, they lived "just up the hill," and it was clear that Johnny's mother never felt that she was more than an outsider. When Johnny was a child and his mother attempted to control his eating by limiting the food that he had available at home, his grandparents would secretively feed him as much candy as he could consume. In fact, they emphasized that it was their secret and that he should never tell his mother.

The mother's parents and father's sisters were also involved in a conspiracy not to disappoint Johnny. It was clear that, wherever he went, someone gave him food. If anything, they forced him to eat rather than tried to help him lose weight. It was clear that the mother's role as the family "bitch" came from her unsuccessful attempts to establish order in a family that gave her no support. The mother, however, did have great difficulty sharing her feelings.

The relationship between mother and son had been very conflictual for many years. Conflicts focused primarily on Johnny's food. He had not learned to drive, and he would beg his mother to go get him some potato chips. She would first refuse, they would argue, and she would go out and come back with two bags of potato chips, one for him and one for the family. Of course, he would eat both bags, another fight would ensue, and she would again go to the grocery store. As Johnny had dropped out of high school at age 16 and never left the house, his failure to do household chores was another source of conflict.

Treatment was directed at the dysfunctional family dynamics and at Johnny's very low self-esteem. It was also necessary to establish a realistic weight loss program for him that could help him regain his confidence and pull him out of the home, where he was at this time virtually a prisoner. A secondary goal of treatment was to help Johnny obtain a driver's license. He had failed his initial test at 16 and was ashamed because he realized he could not read the questions properly. Nutritional control of his eating, structured physical activity, individual therapy, family therapy, and group therapy were all used in treatment.

Johnny's weight gain had resulted primarily from compulsive and continuous snacking. Consequently, the dietary goal was to restrict snacking, while having him eat a reduced diet of approximately 1,800 calories. This was begun immediately and continued throughout the treatment process.

Johnny was so physically disabled that his physical activity program had to progress very slowly. He literally had to rest after walking across the street for his therapy sessions. Despite this, he was required to accomplish a certain amount of physical activity each day. This resulted in a continuous improvement in his stamina and physical strength.

Family therapy had two specific goals. The first was to focus on the mother-son conflict and the effect of the mother-father relationship on it. The father was structurally brought into the family and placed in a more appropriate parental role, by having him monitor the son's behaviors at home and help the son prepare for his driver's test. The mother was also encouraged to make more demands of the father, including a demand that he spend more time with her. This went more slowly than did the weight loss effort, as the mother found it very difficult to relinquish her role as the overburdened martyr of the family. She also had great difficulty in accepting and giving positive support within the family. In one early family session, Johnny gave his mother some mill-ground flour that he had bought for her as a present on a field trip. As she grabbed the bag, she snapped that she could feed the birds with it. In the same session, she also loudly complained that he had not done anything. The therapist pointed out to her that he had actually lost 25 pounds and that she should be proud of his effort.

The members of this family had to learn to demand respect. The parents were brought together structurally by urging the father to support the mother more actively and to demand that Johnny cease his disrespectful behavior. Johnny, in turn, was taught that he could demand respect by behaving differently with other people. The family was brought together as a nuclear unit to support themselves against the intrusions of their other relatives.

In fact, the second major goal of family therapy was to neutralize the behaviors of the extended family that had sabotaged Johnny's success. The father's parents had died, but the mother's mother and the father's sisters were involved in the family therapy process. The goal was to challenge their behaviors and simultaneously to elicit their aid in blocking Johnny's efforts to sabotage his own success. During one of these sessions, Johnny said with a loud curse, "It's not fair. You're cutting off my supply line!" This became the theme of the extended family therapy.

Johnny began to lose weight and feel better physically, he also began to respond to the support of his individual therapist and the group. In both individual therapy and group therapy, the issues of leaving his home and separating from his family of origin were central. Johnny's genogram was examined in the group, and the price that he was paying for not leaving home was noted. The way in which his family kept him at home was also explained to him. As he became more motivated to change, ways that he could sabotage the system in a healthy manner were suggested to him. During this time, his hospital behavior changed from that of a hostile, withdrawn young man to that of a more open and good-humored person.

During the transitional stage, when Johnny was feeling more assertive and in control but his relationship with his mother had not yet changed, he showed his sensitivity to the function of the symptom in the family, at the same time refusing to pay the price that his role had until now demanded. Following both his first and second weekend visits home, his mother announced that things were as bad as ever. She complained that he roamed the house as

in the past, slamming all the cabinet doors, seeking food, and generally making her life miserable. It became clear in the family session, however, that actually many things had changed and that the only remaining negative behavior was the cabinet door banging. Johnny was mimicking his former behavior, allowing his mother the security of being able to complain, but he was refusing to eat the food, allowing himself to be successful in his goal. Johnny admitted that he had been making sandwiches during the second visit home as he had done in the past, which infuriated his mother, but he threw them in the trash can without eating them.

As the mother and father interacted more with each other, the mother began to soften her stance, and Johnny no longer needed to give her something about which to complain. He was now able to associate the family process with his long-standing feelings. For example, he told his parents that, for many years, he had hated his father's silence. The family had developed a pattern over the years in which the mother went out on the weekend and the father was silent; this indicated an impending fight. Johnny became very anxious and worried at these times, and he would eat, eat, and eat.

The therapy had attempted with some success to rejoin Johnny's parents as a functional marital couple and help Johnny achieve a greater sense of autonomy and self-esteem. This was facilitated by his rapid physical improvement and weight loss. All aspects of this process were essential—one could not occur without the others. On discharge from the hospital after a 6-week stay, Johnny had lost 56 pounds. At 6 months' follow-up, he had lost an additional 100 pounds, obtained his driver's license, and was seldom at home. Thus freed, his mother had taken a part-time job and was less depressed and significantly less hostile. The mother and the father were continuing to interact more appropriately.

REFERENCES

Bowen, M. (1978). *Family therapy in clinical practice*. New York: Aronson.

Bruch, H., & Touraine, E. (1940). Obesity in childhood, *V:* The family frame of obese children. *Psychosomatic Medicine, 2,* 141–206.

Fisch, R., Weakland, J., & Segal, L. (1982). *The tactics of change*. San Francisco: Jossey-Bass.

Ganley, R.M. (1985). *Family systems and obesity: Exploration of a psychosomatic model with consideration of the restrained eating dimension.* Unpublished manuscript.

Hall, C.M. (1983). *The Bowen theory and its uses*. New York: Aronson.

Harkaway, J.E. (1983). Obesity: Reducing the larger system. *Journal of Strategic and Systemic Therapies, 2(3),* 2–16.

Harkaway, J.E. (1986). Structural assessment of families with obese adolescent girls. *Journal of Marital and Family Therapy, 12,* 199–201.

Kaufman, G. (1980). *Shame: The power of caring*. New York: Schankman.

LeBow, M.D. (1984). *Child obesity*. New York: Springer.

Madanes, C. (1981). *Strategic family therapy*. San Francisco: Jossey-Bass.

Marshall, J.R., & Neill, J. (1977). The removal of a psychosomatic symptom: Effect on the marriage. *Family Process, 16,* 273–288.

McVoy, J. (1980). *An ethnographic analysis of the family dynamics of obese adolescents.* Unpublished doctoral dissertation, Virginia Polytechnic Institute and State University, Blacksburg, VA.

Minuchin, S., Rosman, B.L., & Baker, L. (1978). *Psychosomatic families: Anorexia nervosa in context*. Cambridge, MA: Harvard University Press.

Penn, P. (1982). Circular questioning. *Family Process, 21,* 265–271.

Polivy, J., & Herman, C. (1983). *Breaking the diet habit*. New York: Basic Books.

Powers, P.S. (1980). *Obesity: The regulation of weight*. Baltimore: Williams & Wilkins.

Rona, E., & Chinn, S. (1982). National study of health and growth: Social and family factors in obesity in primary school children. *Annals of Human Biology, 9,* 131–145.

Stalanos, P.M. (1985). Behavior modification for obesity: The evaluation of exercise, contingency management and program adherence. *Journal of Consulting Clinical Psychology, 46,* 463–469.

Stunkard, A.J. (1980). *Obesity*. New York: Saunders.

Stunkard, A.J. (1984). The current status of treatment for obesity in adults. *Psychiatric Annals, 13,* 862–867.

Subby, R., & Friel, J. (1984). Co-dependency: A paradoxical dependency. In *Co-dependency: An emerging issue*. Pompano Beach, FL: Health Communications.

Vandereycken, W. (1986). Family therapy and eating disorders. *Second International Conference on Eating Disorders*. New York: Albert Einstein College of Medicine.

Wiley, R.B. (1979). *Family systems factors in childhood obesity*. Unpublished doctoral dissertation, Texas Tech University, Lubbock, Texas.

Young, C.M. (1964). Psychologic factors in weight control. *American Journal of Clinical Nutrition, 5,* 186–191.

7

Cybernetic Approaches to Weight Control

Bradford P. Keeney, PhD
Director, Family Therapy Program
Texas Tech University
Lubbock, Texas
   and
Frank N. Thomas, MA
Joseph Strano, MA
Nancy Ridenour, MA
James Morris, MA
Paul N. McKenzie, MA
C. Jefferson Hood, MA
Debra Denman, MA
Brent J. Atkinson, MA
Family Therapy Doctoral Program
Department of Human Development
   and Family Studies
Texas Tech University
Lubbock, Texas

THE TERM *CYBERNETICS* IS generally defined as the science of effective organization (Beer, 1976). The most elementary idea of cybernetics, feedback, refers specifically to the way in which a system uses its outcomes to organize its subsequent behavior (Keeney, 1983a). Therefore, the effective organization of a system is achieved through appropriate forms of feedback that enable a system to correct, organize, and control its own behavior. This elementary cybernetic perspective can be used in the design of clinical strategies to help people effectively control their eating behavior and weight.

The fact that problems are both idiosyncratic and contextual is very evident in the area of weight. A person's weight may or may not be problematic for that particular person and his or her social network, for the judgment of size, weight, and control of weight cannot be defined dichotomously as "healthy" and "pathological/problematic." Viewed with the cybernetic lens, the goal of therapy is not the removal of pathology, but the activation of the order of feedback that the system requires to self-correct. Perhaps the most useful definition of pathology is that it is "escalating sameness" (Keeney, 1983a, p. 126), the maximizing or minimizing of any system variable. With this in mind, the problem (i.e., weight control) can be defined as an attempt of a lower order of the system to be calibrated at a higher level. Intervention, therefore, is complementary to diagnosis, and these should not (and cannot) be divided. If intervention is both the creating and the discerning of difference (Keeney, 1983a), the process of change involves the provision of a change of change (called "sociofeedback'' by Keeney [1983a]), enabling the therapeutic system to "(re)calibrate how it maintains its organization" (Keeney & Ross, 1985, pp. 57–58). From this perspective, the problem of weight control can be addressed in the therapeutic context as any other presenting problem is addressed.

BASIC CYBERNETIC APPROACH TO WEIGHT CONTROL

In our clinical work, we have followed a very simple guideline: we use the outcome of each intervention intended to help a client control his or her weight as a resource in designing the subsequent intervention. This pattern of feedback has the practical effect of connoting all outcomes as positive or useful—they simply provide information for the organization and design of subsequent work. In this regard, our work is part of the class of therapeutic approach sometimes called "systemic therapies" (Keeney & Ross, 1985).

Clients hear about our work through local advertisements on the Cybernetic Weight Control Project. Our target population is clearly defined. We do not generally treat anyone who is a medical risk, although we have worked with a few clients in cooperation with local physicians. For the most part, persons who call the Project are informed that, in order to participate, they must meet the following criteria: they must currently weigh 20 to 50 pounds above their normal weight (e.g., according to actuary tables), and they must be accompanied by the person or persons most interested and involved in their weight control. Our clients range from 12 to 60 years of age,

and nearly all are accompanied by significant others, such as parents, spouses, roommates, close friends, and work colleagues.

We follow this strategy in the general belief that any client system can be used in the process of change. Furthermore, a client's family may not always be the most relevant social context for facilitating therapeutic change. Because we encourage the client's full participation in defining both the problem and the solution(s), it is only natural that the client should choose the social context for change.

New clients usually report a history of many previous efforts to lose weight, often through commercial weight control programs, popular books, or psychotherapy. Many clients have already become diet experts with extensive knowledge about weight reduction programs and know how to lose weight easily, but are frustrated by their failures to maintain weight loss. We subsequently suggest that our efforts will help them learn to *control* their weight rather than to lose weight per se. The first assignment that we give them is paradoxically to gain 2 pounds accurately and carefully in the next week. We explain that, because *control* requires accuracy in both losing and gaining weight, the assignment is simply one way to assess their ability to control their weight. As they have described their efforts to control weight loss, we mention that we want to determine what happens when they try to manage weight gain. This task has the pragmatic consequence of transforming their problem definition of weight loss into a definition of weight control, which provides a therapeutic rationale for prescribing their problem.

The next session focuses strictly on the outcome of the beginning task. Whatever happens, whether it be weight loss, maintenance, or gain, the therapist or therapy team searches for a way to use the outcome as a clue, direction, and resource for the design of the next intervention. In this way, a unique cybernetic strategy for weight control is constructed for each client through the feedback process that links each intervention in a pattern of recursion and self-correction.

The prescription to gain weight carefully and accurately builds a therapeutic reality that is different from most or all of the clients' previous attempts to control weight. The emphasis on the control of weight rather than the loss of weight usually has the intended result of reframing all that is attempted both in and out of sessions as assessment. By making the program idiosyncratic to the client, the therapy not only maintains consistency with the cybernetic training model, but also allows a great deal of ambiguity regarding when treatment begins and assessment ends. The result is a therapy without failures, a change process that uses both weight gain and weight loss indiscriminately in therapy. This may be part of the reason that it is not unusual for a client to stay in the Project for weeks without any weight loss while the team assesses patterns and develops strategies for change.

Interventions can usually be labeled assessment tasks for approximately four to six sessions. We contextualize and explain that these assessment tasks help the client to understand his or her relationship to eating. It is sometimes useful to encourage clients to assess their relationship to eating in ways other than weighing themselves.

One woman was instructed to find three skirts that represented three fitness levels for her—one that presently fit her, one that was a bit too tight, and another that was a bit too large. She was then instructed to assess her progress in terms of the way in which these skirts fit her.

Sometimes a shift in the pattern of assessment itself is enough to disrupt problematic eating sequences.

Other approaches may be used to study a client's binge eating.

A client reported that her greatest pleasure in eating centered around "stuffing food" into her mouth. To assess this more carefully, we suggested that she eat one entire head of lettuce immediately before a binge. This, we explained, would prolong the binge experience so that she could more accurately assess the way in which she was stuffing food into her mouth without the consequence of additional calories. In this case, the client bought eight heads of lettuce, as directed, to be ready for several binges. She ate the first one the evening after the task had been assigned. She found that it short-circuited her enjoyment of eating sweets and found it difficult to binge after she had performed this task only one time.

Another client was instructed to continue her snacking habits, but to make one modification: after a few bites of a snack, she was to wrap up the food immediately and put it aside. Then she was to wait as long as she could, perhaps 20 to 30 minutes, and to think about how good the rest of her snack would taste. After that time, she was to finish eating the snack. When the client reported that this procedure had decreased her snacking, we requested that she try even harder to explore her relationship to eating snacks. This time we focused on her favorite snack—chocolate cake. When she wanted a piece of cake, she was to eat only half a slice, wrap the other half, and place it in the freezer. After 1 week of this, she was told to take a half piece out of the freezer whenever she wanted cake, thaw it, and again concentrate on the experience of eating.

When the client brings other members of his or her social system to a session, we often request their participation in assessing the client's eating behavior. If they are cooperative, we may place them completely in charge of the client's eating habits. Should a client become annoyed by the (over)participation of this person or persons, we design an intervention that uses this outcome.

When a husband was asked to take notes on his wife's eating, she reported having trouble snacking because his presence bothered her. Our next intervention was to make her responsible for diminishing her snacking; however, if she were to begin failing, she was to ask her husband to take over. The woman quickly reduced her snacking binges.

After they have performed a series of assessment tasks, clients sometimes ask to begin working directly on losing weight. We immediately respond that we have been waiting for this request and that we can now move on to the next part of our work. Several classes of interventions are useful at this stage. If there is any ambiguity in a client's proposals about losing weight, we set up another "test" to determine whether he or she is "really" ready to begin a "serious" weight control program. In other cases, we tell the client directly and simply to use whatever diet he or she wants and attempt to lose 2 to 3 pounds every week; we then give the client 2 or 3 weeks to see what happens. Finally, we have used a more indirect and ambiguous form of intervention:

> The team and I feel it's time to tell you what we've been wanting to tell you. It may shock you at first. Sometimes we've been telling you we needed to gather information when we were actually intervening. At other times, we've been gathering information, although you may have thought we were intervening. Other approaches to dieting and weight control have addressed your conscious mind. We, on the other hand, address your unconscious mind. At this time, you have all the pieces you need to control your weight. You may not realize it now, but you will in the weeks to come. You may be surprised at how you will creatively put together all the pieces that are already within you. Call us in 2 weeks about your progress. If you need another session, we'll get the team together again. If we have to, we'll use a stronger intervention, although we'd like to hold off on that.

In sum, the simple idea of feedback is used to construct cybernetic strategies for helping people achieve successful weight control.

CYBERNETIC-CONSTRUCTIVIST TEAM APPROACH TO WEIGHT CONTROL

The Cybernetic Weight Control Project is based on the theoretical idea that therapeutic realities are constructed through the management of semantic and political frames of reference (Keeney & Ross, 1985; Keeney & Silverstein, 1986). Semantic frames of reference are communication contexts that focus principally on the construction and elaboration of meaning, whereas political frames of reference are communication contexts that focus principally on the specifics of social organization (i.e., who is doing what to whom when, where, and how).

The Team Members

When we use a team approach to therapy, we designate one team member as coordinator. At the initial session, this person introduces himself or herself as the coordinator and explains that a variety of specialists will also be working with them, that some of these specialists are observers from behind a one-way mirror, and that each specialist will be introduced when his or her service is needed. Should the clients have any questions about the treatment, they are asked to direct their inquiries to the coordinator. Thus, the coordinator serves as the contact person for the client system, handling all telephone calls from the clients as well as the social greeting at the beginning of each session. In summary, the coordinator takes principal responsibility for joining the client system with the therapist system and ensuring that the organizational flow of a session is smooth and meaningful for the clients.

Other team members take on the specific tasks of constructing semantic and political frames of reference. When the team decides to construct a particular communication frame, such as a view of the interactional pattern associated with the problem eating behavior, the coordi-

nator is called from the room and given the task of introducing a "pattern assessment specialist." This specialist's job is defined as examining the patterns that lead to the person's weight control problem. The name and explanation (semantics) of this team member's task, "pattern assessment," is itself an intervention for both clients and therapists. It provides a specific focus for therapy.

When the specialist in pattern assessment obtains the desired information or if the observing team decides that some other line of inquiry may be more useful, the coordinator is sent into the room to introduce another specialist, such as a meaning assessment specialist. The coordinator then leaves, and the new specialist pursues another focus for questioning. The responses of clients to a team member's efforts to construct a particular communication frame are used to shape the next frame. In this way, the team constructs a unique form of therapeutic reality in each session.

Sometimes a team member is unable to build the intended frame. In this event, another therapist may be sent to ask different questions in an effort to elicit the same information. At other times, a team member constructs a frame that provides clues for the construction of an entirely different class of frame.

In addition to the team members already mentioned, there is a session orchestrator behind the one-way mirror. This person is the communication link between the coordinator and other members of the therapy team. He or she is responsible both for making all calls to the coordinator and for explaining any instructions to the coordinator in regard to particular communication frames and the introduction of assessment specialists.

The Organizational Design

At the beginning of therapy, the coordinator generally explains the structure of treatment to the clients. When the preliminary rituals of introduction have been completed, the coordinator asks three basic questions:

1. What do we need to know about your weight problem?
2. What is the most important thing we need to know about your weight problem?
3. Have you left any important information out?

Clients may answer these questions very briefly and directly, or they may take a long time to tell "their story." The coordinator simply listens and waits until they have stopped talking in response to one question before asking the next question. At this time, the clients are presenting basic frames concerned with semantics and politics.

When all the questions have been answered, the coordinator leaves the room, announcing that he or she will return with a colleague. The coordinator and the observing team meet and discuss which frame to address and/or construct. They may decide to construct a therapeutic contract about the weight or eating problem (semantics) or a frame that identifies the organization of problem eating behavior (political). Following the team's discussion, the orchestrator chooses the appropriate assessment specialist, who is then introduced to the client by the coordinator.

Eventually, a political frame evolves that enables the therapeutic team to suggest interventions that may change a pattern of organization. For example, an organizational pattern may be changed by altering its frequency, rate, duration, time, location, intensity, quality, circumstance, or sequence (O'Hanlon & Wilke, in press). When the team members have agreed on two or three possible ways of changing a pattern area, a different specialist is introduced to the client system. Asking the clients what they think would happen if each of the hypothetical changes in the eating behavior were to occur, this specialist attempts to construct semantic frames about politics. This pre-intervention assessment allows the team to hear and observe the clients' reactions to each of the possible types of intervention.

On the basis of the clients' responses, the therapy team decides whether to choose one of these types of interventions, to combine them, to alter them, or to try another pre-intervention assessment. When they have agreed on a particular intervention, the team members decide whether they have the appropriate semantics to package the intervention as an assignment. If not, a "meanings assessment specialist" may be sent to ask the clients what they think the previously proposed changes mean. The clients' responses are then used in constructing a rationale for intervention (Keeney, 1983a; Keeney & Ross, 1985).

When the team members have decided on the appropriate intervention, either the coordinator or another team member may explain it to the clients. Afterward, it is often useful to have an entirely different team member enter the room, announce that he or she is responsible for keeping a clinical record of their case, and ask the clients to summarize the assignment for the record. Although it is common for a therapist to ask clients to repeat their assignment, the clients' replay is tempered by their awareness that the therapist already knows the assignment. The clients' explanation of their assignment to a newcomer gives the therapist a better sense of the clients' understanding of their task. The coordinator may then provide additional specific instructions to tighten the clients' understanding of the therapeutic task.

Subsequent sessions follow the same four stages:

1. The coordinator asks three questions that are general requests for communication frames, usually tailored to focus on a follow-up of the assignment: (a) "What do we need to know about your assignment?" (b) "What is the most important thing we need to know about your assignment?" and (c) "Did you leave anything important out?"
2. Specialists in pattern and meaning assessment construct semantic and political frames, respectively, until a relevant pattern of the organization of the problem eating behavior for which interventions can be designed emerges.
3. A pre-intervention assessment (semantics about politics) is done to determine the clients' predictions of the results if two or three possible changes in the pattern being examined were to take place.
4. Intervention design, intervention delivery, and intervention checkup are fine-tuned.

All four stages involve patterns of feedback in which the clients' responses shape the therapist's responses. A recursion is thereby established whereby clients direct therapists how to direct clients. In this process of sociofeedback (Keeney, 1983a), clients and therapists co-evolve a therapeutic reality. The recursive cycling of semantic and political frames in sociofeedback constitutes the context of therapeutic change. This recursive process again reminds us that clients help construct their therapists' interventions and that therapists participate in constructing their clients' behavior. Both are recursively interlocked.

ALTERNATE DIRECTIONS

The individual clinician can use the cybernetic approach to weight control that has been outlined as a team approach by marking clear distinctions between roles. For example, as the team approach uses a coordinator to elicit certain initial information from the clients, the individual clinician can clearly seek only the desired information while enacting this role. Likewise, the roles of meaning assessment specialist and pattern assessment specialist can be distinct if clearly demarcated and practiced by a solo clinician. Team members who see clients when there is no team behind the mirror have used a series of chairs and/or clipboards to maintain distinct roles in the therapy room, for example. If using separate chairs, the therapist can take a certain chair on entering the room and begin to elicit information using the three initial questions. The therapist can then switch chairs to begin assessments. When the clinician feels that he or she has enough information to begin building ideas about possible interventions, the clinician can leave the room to select two or three possible interventions, returning to carry out the tasks of the remaining stages of therapy.

Another variation has been developed for a team of two members who see two client systems simultaneously in separate rooms. Two therapists whose offices are near each other, for example, can use the team approach by dividing the roles between them. One can be the coordinator and meaning assessment specialist, while the other can be the pattern assessment specialist and the record keeper. They can change roles for each client system, or they can continue in the same roles for all client systems in order to avoid confusion. The two therapists can meet at appointed times in a third room to discuss proposed interventions, to fine-tune interventions, and to sort out meaning assessments. This two-person approach has been used comfortably and successfully by members of the Project team.

Our clients have been enthusiastic about the cybernetic approach. The building of a therapeutic rationale is important for such acceptance, however. We typically approach all weight control clients whom we see in teams (whether the team consists of two or ten) with two basic semantic frames: (1) we normally use several team specialists who enter and leave the therapy room as needed; and (2) it is to the client system's advantage to have such a team, for "several heads are better than one."

OUTCOMES

Our cybernetic approaches to working with weight control clients suggest that outcomes can be divided into four general categories with respect to the semantics and politics of therapy:

1. *semantics same/politics same*. Clients report no alternative understanding of the situation and no difference in eating behavior. This outcome is traditionally described as a "therapeutic failure," although we have proposed that such an outcome is simply information that can be used to construct an alternative strategy.

2. *semantics change/politics same*. Clients present a different understanding of their relationship to food and weight, but report no change in the organization of their eating. For example, clients may decide that they no longer want to have a slim figure and that eating is a form of pleasure worth the retention or addition of extra pounds.

3. *semantics same/politics change*. Clients' patterns of eating change, but no new understandings are reported.

4. *semantics change/politics change*. Clients' understanding of eating changes, as does the contextual organization of eating behavior.

These outcomes refer to the *client's* semantics and politics. Practitioners can examine their own semantic and political frames about a case and determine whether they are changing. Such a perspective would permit subsequent comparisons of the emergence and evolution of the client's semantics and politics with the emergence and evolution of the practitioner's semantics and politics. The nature of "outcome" from this double view would be approached as a co-construction of clients and practitioners. Again, we find our strategies and understanding of outcome to be a consequence of cybernetic feedback, reminding us that the end of treatment is fundamentally (co)constructed in the same fashion as the beginning of treatment.

REFERENCES

Beer, S. (1976). In K. Wilson (Ed.), *The collected works of the biological computer laboratory* (p. 290). Peoria, IL: Illinois Blueprint Company.

Keeney, B.P. (1983a). *Aesthetics of change*. New York: Guilford Press.

Keeney, B.P. (1983b). Ecological assessment. In B.P. Keeney (Ed.), *Diagnosis and assessment in family therapy* (pp. 156–169). Rockville, MD: Aspen Publishers.

Keeney, B.P., & Ross, J.M. (1985). *Mind in therapy: Constructing systemic family therapies*. New York: Basic Books.

Keeney, B.P., & Silverstein, O. (1986). *The therapeutic voice of Olga Silverstein*. New York: Guilford Press.

O'Hanlon, B., & Wilke, J. *Shifting contexts*. New York: Guilford Press.

8

Family Intervention in the Treatment of Childhood and Adolescent Obesity

Jill Elka Harkaway, EdD
Departments of Pediatrics and
  Psychiatry
Tufts Medical School/New England
  Medical Center
Boston, Massachusetts

DESPITE EXTENSIVE RE- search, success rates remain low in the treatment of childhood obesity (Dietz, 1983). One limitation of conventional treatment has been its focus on the individual as the unit of intervention. Recent developments in behavioral treatment that includes family members (Epstein, Wing, Steranchak, Dixon & Michelson, 1980; Epstein, Wing, Koeske, Andrasik, & Ossip, 1981; Brownell, Kelman, & Stunkard, 1983) and the application of family systems theory to obesity (Harkaway, 1983, 1986; Barbarin & Tirado, 1984; Ganley, 1985) are enlarging the focus of treatment, however. While it is useful to redefine the problem as contextual, it is important to remember that obesity is also a physiological condition. Thus, treatment of obesity is most likely to be effective if it addresses both the contextual and the physiological aspects of the problem. With this perspective in mind, I have worked with a pediatrician/nutritionist for the past 3 years in developing a program for the family treatment of obesity that integrates the systemic and medical aspects of childhood and adolescent obesity. The program is based in the pediatric department of a major teaching hospital. Because it is a tertiary care facility, many of our referrals are the most "difficult" patients to treat, but we also receive a large number of self-referrals from the community. Patients range in age from 6 months to 24 years, in weight from 120% to 250% of ideal body weight. We see members of all socioeconomic groups, and we see the

The author gratefully acknowledges William H. Dietz, MD, Ph.D., Director of the Weight Control Program, Tufts/New England Medical Center, Boston.

same number of male and female patients.

When families call the clinic for an appointment, they are scheduled for a two-part intake appointment: 1 hour with the physician for a medical examination, 1 hour with the therapist for a family meeting. The family is seen first by the physician, who takes a family and patient medical history, dietary history, and treatment history. The physical evaluation includes a review of systems and measurements of blood pressure, height, weight, triceps skinfold measurement, and midarm circumference. The physician establishes the patient's ideal body weight (according to height/weight growth charts) and rules out both congenital (e.g., Prader-Willi syndrome) and acquired (e.g., brain tumor or Cushing's disease) medical causes of the obesity. Laboratory tests are also performed (e.g., complete blood count with differential, urinalysis, cholesterol level determination).

The second part of the evaluation is the family interview, which includes as many of the significant members of the family system as possible. If patients come in without parents or other key family members, the interview is rescheduled, and the family is told that treatment cannot be initiated until the family meeting is held. The family interview is used to evaluate whether the patient is likely to lose weight or whether the obesity is such a central part of the family's current interactions that treatment will either fail or be abandoned. During the initial interview, we also explore and attempt to define the system that is organized around the obesity; the family members in this system are invited to return for the next meeting.

At the end of the two-part intake session, we meet briefly to decide how to proceed with the treatment. Families are initially assigned to one of three treatment "protocols" in this informal triage: dietary intervention without further family intervention, family therapy without dietary intervention, or a combination of dietary and family therapy. The decision is based on a number of criteria that predict difficulty in treatment: severity of the obesity, previous attempts at weight loss, and the degree to which the child's obesity seems to be an integral part of the family's interactions. We remain flexible about this initial decision, occasionally shifting the treatment plan to adapt to new information from the family. If dietary intervention is ineffective, the family is referred for further family work; if issues around the child's obesity are resolved, the physician prescribes a dietary intervention, if necessary.

FAMILY ASSESSMENT

Assessment explores three areas: patterns of interactional behavior involving the obesity; beliefs about the problem; and hypotheses about the possible functions of the problem within the system. In considering these three areas, it becomes clear that it may be more difficult for the family to change than to live with the symptom. Ironically and unfortunately, while the symptom may function as a "solution" to dilemmas facing the family, it simultaneously prevents a more constructive resolution. In a systemic model, it is assumed that the family is stuck in these dysfunctional patterns not because of hostility or deficits, but because it does not have within its repertoire solutions that are less toxic.

With obesity, it is not a question of the child's motivation to lose weight or "sabotage" on the part of the family. Rather, the behavior of the individual is constrained by the rules of the system.

Patterns of Interactional Behavior

Families can be divided into five groups that represent general types of interactional patterns: (1) two-parent families in which the parents are in conflict about the child's weight, (2) single-parent families in which the parent is not involved in his or her family of origin, (3) two-parent families in which the parents are united about the child's weight, (4) three-generational families, and (5) families that do not define the child's weight as a problem.

1. In two-parent families, the parents are in disagreement. Parents may disagree either covertly or overtly about the child's weight. One parent may think it a serious problem, while the other thinks "she's fine the way she is; leave her alone." In other cases, the parents may agree about the problem, but have different beliefs about appropriate treatment. This situation can develop into what Minuchin (Minuchin, Rosman, & Baker, 1978) referred to as triangulation. The child becomes caught in a double bind, as the parents demand mutually exclusive behaviors.

In one such family, both parents had been overweight, and both had lost weight. Each had lost weight in a different way, however, and each believed that his or her way was the right approach for their daughter. The father told her to forget about dieting, eat whatever she wanted, and jog every day, that being the way

he lost weight. The mother said she should follow a strict diet and not exercise until she had lost some weight, her method. There was little the daughter could do without betraying one of her parents. If she dieted and lost weight, she proved her father wrong; if she did not diet, but exercised and lost weight, she proved her mother wrong. When she came to the program, she was doing the only thing she could to maintain her loyalty to both; try and fail at everything equally.

This pattern also exists in families in which the parents are separated or divorced. Different eating styles and the possible involvement of step-parents in separate households complicate the situation even further.

2. The single parent who is not involved with his or her family of origin lacks support and extrafamilial resources. This parent may be overwhelmed by the child's behavior. Eating is often one of several uncontrollable behaviors. The parent and the child act as peers and resemble a married couple. Frequently, the child sleeps with the mother and spends all his or her time at home, keeping the mother company. They are socially isolated and totally dependent on each other for companionship.

3. In two-parent families in which the parents are united in their beliefs about the child's weight and its treatment, the conflict about weight occurs between the parents and the child. The parents struggle to help their child lose weight, and the child either rebels openly by refusing to diet or rebels covertly by trying to lose weight but "failing." The parents attempt to cure the child, and the child defeats or refuses them. The parents oscillate between worry and angry frustration. The parent-child conflict may "detour" conflict between the parents, as Minuchin suggested (1978), allowing them to perceive themselves as united in opposition to a common enemy. In any case, the triad becomes locked in a sequence in which the more the parents attempt to help the child, the more the child fails.

4. Families in which three generations are actively involved with each other as a nuclear family are usually single-parent families. There is frequently a struggle between the mother and the grandparent about the child, and this struggle becomes centered around the child's weight. The child is in a cross-generational alliance with a grandparent against the mother, causing the mother to appear incompetent or inadequate. The grandparent criticizes the mother for allowing the child to gain weight or, conversely, for not feeding the child enough. The mother criticizes the grandparent for undermining her authority and feeding the child, but avoids a confrontation with the grandparent about the problem.

5. Some families do not define the child's weight as a problem, but seek treatment because they are referred by a professional. The child's obesity may be mild, and the family's lack of concern a reasonable response; on the other hand, the child may be severely obese, and the lack of concern may in fact be endangering the child's health. In any case, the key interactional problem may be the conflict between the family and the referral source. Treatment must initially address the family–referral source system and its involvement in the maintenance of the problem.

Belief Systems

Patterns of interaction are framed, influenced, and maintained by the family's beliefs. The beliefs that a family has as individuals and as a whole may make it difficult to change the behaviors that are maintaining problems. The beliefs explored in the treatment of obesity relate to the family's definition of the problem (e.g., its severity, causality, and volition) and the family's view of appropriate treatment (e.g., should it be handled by the family or by professionals? what is the most useful treatment? what is the family's history with professional treatment?). This highlights differences between family members and identifies possible sources of conflict. It also helps the therapist or physician to understand that not all family members think the weight a problem and treatment a good thing.

Hypotheses about the Function of the Symptom

Excess weight may become a focus of attention for the family and may solve family dilemmas in many ways. For example, obesity can protect family boundaries by delaying the child's development. In many of these families, the strongest emphasis is placed on loyalty to the family. Family members tend to be overinvolved with each other, but socially isolated. The outside world is seen as a dangerous and hostile place, somehow foreign. Children who feel a strong primary loyalty to their families can be torn between their loyalty and their interest in involvement with peers, particularly as they enter adolescence.

Obesity partially solves this dilemma by keeping the child isolated from the peer group; it becomes the rationale for staying close to home. As the lesser of two evils, obesity relieves the family of the difficulties involved with developmental transitions.

The mother of a massively obese 16-year-old boy who was suffering from high blood pressure, sleep apnea, and other respiratory problems resulting from his obesity said, "We're worried that he's so sick, but at least he's not in trouble with sex and drugs."

Similarly, the child may gain weight and stop going out after one of the parents becomes depressed or suffers a loss. Obesity provides an excuse to stay home and keep an eye on that parent, while providing a focus for the parent's attention.

In one family, the daughter, who had been overweight for some time, decided she was too fat to go out socially anymore and stayed home (eating more and, therefore, getting fatter) shortly after her mother became depressed. The following is taken from a transcript of the first interview:

Therapist: What would you do differently if you lose weight?

Daughter: I would go out more.

Therapist: Who would miss having you around if you did?

Daughter (looks at mother): I don't know. My mother, I guess.

Therapist: What would change for your mother if she missed you?

Daughter (pause): I don't know. *(pause)* Get more depressed, I guess.

Therapist: What are you afraid would happen if she did?

Sister: Maybe she'd have to go in the hospital.

The daughter's obesity appeared to be her attempt to protect her mother, both by giving her something to do and by providing a "watch" for her.

Concern about obesity can keep a conflicted or otherwise distant family together.

In one family in which the parents were divorced, the daughter started to overeat and gain weight shortly after the birth of the father's new baby. The parents had maintained a pseudo-marriage, although they were divorced and the father had remarried. With the birth of the new child, however, the father became more involved with his second family and more disengaged from the first. The mother reported feeling very depressed and "empty" until the daughter started to gain a disturbing amount of weight. At that point, she found herself having long conversations with her ex-husband, who became reinvolved with his first family because of concern about the daughter's weight. In this way, the daughter's weight allowed the family to continue its myth of itself as an intact unit—as long as the daughter remained overweight.

In many families, the onset of the obesity occurs at a time of major crisis or upheaval in the family, such as a death, divorce, or relocation. Other families choose to seek treatment for a child who has been overweight for some time, at a point of transition. An intensified focus on the obesity, if not the obesity itself, becomes functional as a distraction from more serious or painful issues. The focus on weight and the attempt to solve the problem become a way of organizing and uniting family members during the transition.

One family sought treatment of the older daughter's mild obesity shortly after terminal cancer was diagnosed in the youngest child. The older daughter had not gained weight suddenly; it was the family situation that prompted the involvement in treatment.

When all family members are fat or define themselves as fat, obesity can be a mark of loyalty and membership. Many families have a long, multigenerational history of both obesity and unsuccessful attempts at weight loss. To diet unsuccessfully and to continue to struggle may also show loyalty and identification. To lose weight successfully is a statement of individuation in such a family. Because loyalty is the highest value, weight loss can be viewed as betrayal and separation from the family unit.

A 380-pound adolescent boy was brought for treatment only after he developed high blood pressure. Neither he nor his family had ever requested help for his weight before then. Not only were all family members fat, but also they referred to each other with affectionate nicknames related to their obesity, such as Uncle Moose, Tootsie Roll, and Twinkie. Furthermore, one of the boy's uncles had held a world record as one of the fattest men who had ever lived, a fact of which the entire family was very proud. For this boy to lose weight would have been a powerful message of difference to the family, a message likely to be interpreted as rejection or betrayal. Thus, the boy's continued obesity could be perceived as a statement of support, approval, and respect for his family, as well as a visible declaration of membership.

In a number of families, there is one thin and one obese parent. Frequently, the obesity has been a source of conflict in the marriage, with the thin spouse attempting to ''cure'' the obese one. The thin spouse may be exasperated with the problem and insist that it is a simple problem with a simple solution, implying that the other is not motivated or does not have moral strength. The more the thin spouse minimizes the problem or blames the obese spouse, the more the obese spouse must prove that the problem is insoluble. A child's weight gain serves a number of functions in this family. First, it can serve as a visible mark of loyalty to the obese parent, and it is usually that parent with whom the child is aligned (Harkaway, 1986). Second, if the child struggles to lose weight and fails, the failure proves the obese parent's argument that obesity is a difficult problem to solve. Third, the child becomes triangulated in the parents' marriage and provides a way for the parents to continue their conflict, but at a safer distance.

In one family, the thin father would say to his obese daughter "You'd better lose weight if you ever want to get married. Men don't find fat women attractive." To which the obese mother would respond, "Don't worry, dear, any man worth having will love you no matter what you weigh."

This places the child in a delicate position. Not only could weight loss be considered a betrayal of the obese parent, but also it leaves the parents to fight with each other directly.

Obesity can be a form of pseudo-rebellion, an attempt at autonomy without individuation. By defying the parents and refusing to lose weight, the child maintains the illusion that he or she is rebelling. All the while, however, the rebellion keeps the child paradoxically overinvolved with the parents.

Most treatment models do not take into account the function that obesity may play within families. Although undesirable, obesity may come to have a meaning and a place within the system. Because of this, treatment separate from the family relationships may end in failure. Exploring the connectedness of the problem to other parts of the system provides an appreciation of the enormously complex aspects of the problem. It is rather like grabbing hold of a thread and finding that it is part of an intricately woven tapestry.

THE FIRST INTERVIEW

Assessment is an ongoing process that is inseparable from treatment. Nev-ertheless, the first interview provides sufficient information to make decisions about initiating treatment. The format is based on the circular interview developed by the Milan group and is based on the principles of hypothesizing, circularity, and neutrality (Selvini et al, 1980).*

The therapist first asks how the family decided to seek treatment: Who decided who should come and why? If they were referred by an extrafamilial source, what is their view of the referral and their response to it? The referral process critically affects treatment; the family's presence in the clinic may not mean that they want treatment (Harkaway, 1986b).

The second area explored is the reason that the family is seeking treatment at this time. Obesity is rarely an acute problem; most patients who come to the clinic have been overweight for some time. Therefore, there is likely to be another problem within the system that compels the family to seek treatment. The therapist investigates by asking questions. Are there other family problems or stresses on the family at this time? What changes have occurred within the family over the last year? Births? Deaths? Marriages? Divorces? Separations? Illness? Relocation? Job changes? If they were not worried about the weight at this time, what would they be worried about? If they did not come in for treatment, what would happen? Have there been any other problems with this child? Behavioral? Medical? Social? Academic?

The therapist must determine who constitutes the significant system. Who are the people involved in this problem,

---

*I have also been influenced by the work of Imber-Black, 1983; Tomm, 1985, 1986.

and in what way are they involved? The significant system may include not only immediate family, but also extended family and professionals. On occasion, treatment has involved social workers, school counselors, and pediatricians—if not actually in the room, then in the way the therapists think about their role in the system. The question *Who is most worried about your weight?* is helpful in determining not only who is involved, but also how. Who is worried? Who is least worried? Who talks to whom about it? Who tries to help and how? What do others think and say about your weight? Whose fault do they think it is?

Next, the therapist explores definitions of the problem. Who thinks it is a serious problem? Who thinks it is less serious? What is their explanation of the problem? Why, of all their children, is this the only one with a weight problem? In what ways is the obesity a problem? How do they think the child's life would be different if he or she lost weight?

The therapist then asks other questions to explore the history of the problem. When did the child start to gain weight? Who first noticed it? When did they start to think it was a problem? Is weight a family theme? Who else has been overweight? Who has been concerned about weight? (It is important to introduce these as separate issues.) What have they done about the weight?

It is also necessary to ask about previous attempted solutions. What have the family members tried in the past to solve the problem within the family? with outside help? What has been the most/least helpful? How have they responded to intervention/attempts to resolve the problem? What has been the nature of previous attempts at treatment? What are

their beliefs about appropriate treatment at this point? Who thinks they should be seeing a professional, and who thinks they should handle it by themselves? What are the behavioral sequences around the weight and eating behavior? What do other people do? If you were on a diet and your mother saw you eating something you were not supposed to have, what would your mother do? Your father? Your grandmother? If you wanted something to eat that you were not supposed to have, who would you go to? This line of questioning generally reveals cross-generational alliances or coalitions.

Last, the therapist asks questions aimed at the development of hypotheses about the function of the problem. What is possible in this family because of the obesity? What can be avoided because of it? Who is closer or more distant because of it? The therapist asks the family several types of questions. If the child lost weight, how would his relationship with his father (mother, sister, grandfather, etc.) change? Would they spend more or less time together? Would they fight more or less? How would things change in other relationships? What would you talk about if you did not have to talk about his weight? What would you do that you cannot do now?

In order to explore the negative consequences of weight loss, the therapist may begin by stating that everyone always focuses on the positive results of weight loss, but no one ever looks at its cost. The therapist expresses concern that family members are unprepared to deal with the unpleasant aftereffects, adding that they need to know what might happen if the child loses weight. When they are asked to think about the negative consequences that the child's success might have for them, their responses frequently include an increase in social activity, such as dating.

TREATMENT

Our treatment program is based on a systemic epistemology and family intervention. Because the obesity is viewed in terms of its connectedness to the family, individual members and relationships, history, behavior, and beliefs, interventions are directed at the context, not at the problem or the individual members. In addition, it is understood that family intervention does not always involve family therapy. Not all families with obese children are dysfunctional, and not all cases of obesity are evidence of family pathology. Many obese children come from well-adjusted functional families and are themselves normal and happy children.

The first interview, although defined as an assessment, is an important part of the treatment. During this interview, a working relationship is established and a therapeutic framework introduced. For families who receive dietary intervention only, this may be the only formal family session in their treatment. It is important, however, as it defines the problem and its solution within the family context. It provides an opportunity to explore the problem and may encourage the family to work together more effectively. It also allows family members to participate in the design of the treatment plans that will influence their daily lives. For some families, it is the first time that they discuss the problem with each other openly. Others report that it is the first time that they have ever talked to each other about their feelings and beliefs.

Dietary Intervention Only

Involving visits with the physician only, dietary intervention is prescribed for families in which the obesity is not severe (beyond 150%), there have been no previous attempts at weight loss, and the obesity appears to have no significant meaning or function within the family system.

An Italian immigrant family came to the clinic with an overweight son and daughter because the school guidance counselor had expressed concern that the children's weight would prove a social handicap. The family consisted of two parents, both of whom were significantly overweight, and their three children. The youngest, a 2-year-old, was also overweight. No one in the family had ever attempted to lose weight before, nor had anyone considered the weight a problem until the school referral. Both parents now realized that Americans had different ideas about weight than did the people in their village in Italy. The family appeared healthy and flexible in their interactions with each other, and the obesity seemed irrelevant to all their relationships. It was hypothesized that simple dietary intervention, with some instruction about caloric diet, would be helpful. The family undertook a weight reduction diet with no further family intervention. All members lost a significant amount of weight.

Dietary intervention takes the form of a reduction in or elimination of certain foods, as opposed to a structured diet. Those who are trying to lose weight are less likely to adhere to structured diets because of boredom, the impracticality of the diets, and a sense of restriction/deprivation. Because fats are a major source of calories in children, as are "junk" foods, these foods are most frequently modified. Because TV viewing is also highly correlated with obesity (Dietz & Gortmacher, 1985), a reduction in viewing time and an increase in physical activity are recommended.

Family Therapy

When the obesity appears to have a significant meaning and/or major function within the system, and there have been numerous attempts at weight reduction, dietary intervention appears to be doomed from the start. Family therapy without dietary intervention is initiated in these families. When the family is seen only in family therapy, they meet with the therapist at regular intervals, although rarely more frequently than every 2 or 3 weeks. This timing is determined in part by a theoretical position that therapy can be more effective when there is sufficient time between sessions for the family to respond to the intervention (Selvini, 1983). Meetings that are too frequent can put too much emphasis on weight loss, causing the patient to attempt to lose weight too quickly.

Family therapy with dietary intervention is our most common treatment approach. The prescription of dietary and behavioral changes is an intervention into the system that makes it possible to observe the family's response. It highlights transactions within the family around the weight and helps the therapist to plan the next move in therapy (Dietz, 1983). When the therapy includes dietary intervention, patients are followed by the physician at 6- to 8-week intervals for medical follow-up and modification of dietary prescriptions.

The current treatment model for obesity is based on a theoretical framework of Milan systemic therapy that incorporates structural and strategic interventions. This model allows the most flexibility with a very rigid problem, such as obesity, and has proved much more effective over time. The two key elements and foundation of the treatment model are the therapeutic stance of neutrality and the process of circular questioning.

Neutrality (Selvini et al., 1980) is the nonjudgmental stance held by the therapist toward individuals, behaviors, and beliefs. It is a position of inquiry that compels the therapist to understand the ways in which the system functions and, in this instance, the ways in which the obesity is connected to all other parts of the system. Neutrality is of particular importance in the treatment of obesity, because obesity provokes such intense moralistic and judgmental responses from others. For this reason, a position that does not define obesity as pathological is in itself a powerful intervention; neutrality toward the definition of obesity introduces the notion that pathology is arbitrarily defined and challenges the family's beliefs. When did you start to believe that his weight was a problem? Who gave you the idea that you needed to do something about it? In what ways is the weight a problem? What else would be lost if she lost weight? What if he lost weight, and he still had low self-esteem?

Finally, the therapist tries to be neutral about outcome. There are many possible positive outcomes of treatment; weight loss is one of them, but it is not always the best.

One example of the way neutrality is used in treatment is the management of weighing in. I weigh each child at the beginning of each session and then have the child report back to the family in the therapy room. I do not give positive or negative reinforcement to the child about the weight, but ask questions of the family pertaining to this information: are you surprised? If you knew he or she had gained/lost, how did you know? Which of your parents do you think is most upset/angry/happy? The information is used to explore the responses of the system, and to shift the focus from the weight to relationships. A position of curiosity, not judgment, is maintained.

Circular questions (Tomm 1985, 1986; Penn 1982) are useful both to gather information from the family and to introduce new information. When used properly, circular questions challenge family members' beliefs and allow them to think differently about themselves. For example, in asking questions about negative consequences, the therapist can challenge the belief that obesity is bad and suggest that there might be valid, if dysfunctional, reasons for the problem. Circular questions also highlight the ways in which the obesity is connected to other aspects of family's life. They allow for different definitions of the problem and, therefore, for different solutions.

Beyond these two guidelines, each therapy is designed to meet the idiosyncratic needs of the family. The emphasis is on the ability of the therapist to think systemically and to conduct a systemic interview.

CONCLUSION

We are currently compiling data for an outcome study of the patients treated in the 3 years that this program has been in operation. At this point, we know that our success rate with weight loss doubled (from 11% to 22%) within the first year of the introduction of family therapy (Dietz, 1983). We also have a great deal of anecdotal data; a number of grossly obese adolescents who had been given up as hopeless cases have lost a significant amount of weight over the last 2 years. We suspect that we have a lower dropout rate than the norm, despite the fact that our treatment requires participation of family members who may have to miss work and travel some distance.

One of the most interesting aspects that we are exploring in our follow-up study is the definition of success. Weight loss is one significant measure of success, the one most frequently used. Other life changes, such as improved social, academic, and behavioral functioning, are also important indicators of change within the system, however. We see families in which there is an intense over-focus on a child's mild or even moderate obesity. If a family such as this decides to discontinue treatment and no longer defines the weight as a problem, we would consider it successful treatment. Clearly, the measurement of outcome is more complex than the number of pounds lost, and we are working at this point to develop an outcome measure that will address this issue.

REFERENCES

Barbarin, O., & Tirado, M. (1984). Family involvement and successful treatment of obesity: A review. *Family Systems Medicine, 2*(1) 37–45.

Brownell, K., Kelman, J., & Stunkard, A. (1983). Treatment of obese children with and without their mothers: Changes in weight and blood pressure. *Pediatrics, 71*(4), 515–523.

Dietz, W.H., Jr. (1983). Childhood obesity: Susceptibility, cause, and management. *Journal of Pediatrics, 103*(5), 676–686.

Dietz, W.H., Jr. & Gortmacker, S.L. (1985). Do we fatten our children at the television set? Obesity and television viewing in children and adolescents. *Pediatrics, 75*(5), 807–812.

Epstein, L.H., Wing, R.R., Steranchak, L., Dixon, B., & Michelson, J. (1980). Comparison of family-based behavioral modification and nutritional education for childhood obesity. *Journal of Pediatric Psychology, 5,* 25–36.

Epstein, L., Wing, R.R., Koeske, R. Andrasik, F., & Ossip, D. (1981). Child and parent weight loss in family-based behavior modification programs. *Journal of Consulting and Clinical Psychology, 49*(5), 674–685.

Ganley, R. (1985). Family systems and obesity: Exploration of a psychosomatic model with consideration of the restrained eating dimension. Unpublished manuscript.

Harkaway, J.E. (1983). Obesity: Reducing the larger system. *Journal of Strategic and Systemic Therapies.* 2(3), 2–16.

Harkaway, J.E. (1986). Structural assessment of families with obese adolescent girls. *Journal of Marital and Family Therapy, 12*(2), 199–201.

Harkaway, J.E. (in press). Chronic obesity: A systemic approach to medical non-compliance.

Imber-Black (Coppersmith), E. (1983). The family and public sector systems: Interviewing and interventions. *Journal of Strategic and Systemic Therapies,* 85–99.

Imber-Black (Coppersmith), E. (1983). The family and public service systems: An assessment method. In B. Keeney (Ed.), *Diagnosis and assessment in family therapy.* (pp. 38–47). Rockville, MD: Aspen Publishers.

Minuchin, S., Rosman, B., & Baker, L. (1978). *Psychosomatic families: Anorexia nervosa in context.* Boston: Harvard University Press, 1978.

Penn, P. (1982). Circular questioning. *Family Process, 21*(3), 267–280.

Selvini-Palazzoli, M. (1983). Why a long interval between sessions—The therapeutic control of the family-therapist suprasystem. In Andolfi & Zwerling (Eds.), *Dimensions of family therapy* (pp. 161–170). New York: Guilford Press.

Selvini-Palazzoli, M., Boscolo, L., Cecchin, G., & Prata, G. (1980). Hypothesizing-circularity-neutrality: Three guidelines for the conductor of the session. *Family Process, 19,* 3–12.

Tomm, K., (1985). Circular interviewing: A multifaceted clinical tool. In Campbell & Draper (Eds.), *Applications of systemic family therapy: The Milan Method* (pp. 33–45). New York: Academic Press.

Tomm, K. (in press). Interventive Interviewing: Part I. Strategizing as a fourth guideline for the therapist. *Family Process.*

9

Integrating Family and Individual Therapy for Anorexia Nervosa

John Sargent, MD
Director
Eating Disorders Program
Philadelphia Child Guidance Clinic
  and
Clinical Assistant Professor of
  Psychiatry and Pediatrics
University of Pennsylvania School of
  Medicine
Philadelphia, Pennsylvania

MICHELLE, AGED 14, WAS IN the ninth grade. She lived with her parents and her 13-year-old sister. She had been losing weight over the past 6 months and now weighed 88 pounds. Her mother was a talented computer engineer who had recently resumed work. Although her father had a congenital weakness of his legs that made it difficult for him to walk, even with crutches, he had been quite successful as an accountant. The family had recently moved to a new community, and Michelle was having difficulty socially in her new school.

Michelle was described as serious and intense, quiet and also friendly, but rarely outspoken before her weight loss. She had always been a shy and studious girl, but she had made some friends and had attempted to be active, especially in sports. Her younger sister, who was more aggressive socially and athletically, had presented more problems for her parents in raising her. Michelle had reacted to difficulties in family life, such as her father's disappointment with his physical condition, her mother's frustration when not working, or her parents' problems with her younger sister, by being more dutiful around the house and more responsive to other family members. Michelle's weight loss began gradually, but increased steadily. Her parents identified the problem rapidly and sought help through their physician. When psychotherapy was suggested, the parents reviewed several options and made arrangements to begin treatment within a 2-week period of time.

Martha, aged 16, had been underweight for the past 16 months. She lived with her father, new stepmother, two sisters, and a brother in a rural area. Her natural mother lived in the neighboring town. Before her parents' separation, Martha's family had lived for 5 years in South America, where both parents had been missionaries. Following the family's return to their home, the mother soon became anorectic, lost 30 pounds, regained her weight, and left home shortly thereafter, leaving the children in the care of their father. The father remarried, and Martha began to lose weight.

The mother resumed regular contact with the children only after Martha's initial weight loss. A great deal of hostility remained between Martha's parents, who interacted irregularly and treated each other with marked distrust and mutual disrespect. The mother felt that the father had not allowed her space within the family, and the father felt that the mother had been destructive and sinful in leaving the family. Martha not only persisted in her dieting, but also began to go through periods of bingeing and purging. Despite three hospitalizations, she had reached her lowest weight—63 pounds. Both her mother and father remained involved with Martha, but they were unable to cooperate, each accusing the other of sabotaging treatment or being to blame for Martha's difficulties. The entire family, together with the mother's new boyfriend, felt terrified and hopeless; they had no idea how to proceed.

Jennifer, aged 19, was a sophomore at a university 100 miles from her home. She had been anorectic for the past 4 years, with her weight fluctuating between 85 and 95 pounds. She was the youngest of four daughters and had always been viewed as the baby in the family. She saw herself as close to both her parents. She was similar in temperament to her father, a successful attorney who was prone to fits of self-criticism and doubt. She was caring toward her mother, a bright and successful woman who was deeply distressed by behavior problems that her third daughter had developed as well as by Jennifer's anorexia.

Jennifer had become anorectic shortly after an automobile accident that had occurred when she was with her parents. The damage to the car had been major, and Jennifer had been trapped in the back seat. Her father had first freed her mother from the car and then gone back to rescue Jennifer. Jennifer had been afraid that she might die, had felt abandoned by her parents, and had been furious with herself because she had been unable to free herself. She had vowed to herself that she would never again be so vulnerable. Her anorexia was part of her attempt following the accident to make herself strong, self-reliant, and independent. The automobile accident had colored the family's life for quite some time, making them all aware of their vulnerability and mutual dependence.

The three older daughters subsequently left home to attend college. Jennifer's father became more self-absorbed and unhappy, and Jennifer's relationship with her mother intensified around Jennifer's anorexia. She had seen two therapists without making much progress, but she had been able to finish high school successfully and to complete her first year at college with some difficulty. She talked with her parents by telephone several times a week, discussing her moods, her weight, and her eating disorder. Jennifer also remained aware of her sister's difficulties and the distress that those problems caused her mother. She continued to be her mother's confidant concerning these difficulties. She had also begun steadily dating a young man in her college class.

Erica, aged 27, had lived in Europe for the previous 2½ years. She had been anorectic for 8½ years, with wide fluctuations in her weight. In addition, she had serious difficulties with drug and alcohol abuse. She had also gone on regular spending sprees that left her in debt. She was the third of six children in a prominent family. Her parents had divorced when she was 11, and, over the next 4 years, she had been her mother's primary friend, care-giver, and confidant. She had remained in contact with her father, but she was quite disdainful of his behavior and life style; however, she also deeply respected his accomplishments and successes. Erica, an extremely accomplished tennis player, had completed college at a prestigious university. In the years following college, she had worked at a number of jobs. Her mother had remarried and moved

several thousand miles from the family's original place of residence, leaving Erica on her own.

Everyone in the family knew that Erica was having problems, but expected that she would resolve them on her own and that everything would be fine if only she would eat normally. No help was sought, but ultimately an aunt tried to help by inviting Erica to come and live with her. Things improved for Erica over the next year. The aunt died suddenly, however, and Erica's eating disorder returned. Her oldest brother finally brought her back to the family's home when she was extremely ill and near death. Erica agreed to medical hospitalization and to outpatient psychotherapy, but would not agree to psychiatric hospitalization. She requested individual psychotherapy rather than family therapy and agreed to work to pay for her treatment.

These four cases demonstrate the range of difficulties that challenge the therapist who works with anorectics and their families. There are similarities among the four cases: each family is undergoing serious stress; each young woman is in an important position within the family and has demonstrated ability, as well as marked concern for the well-being of her parents; each has an opportunity, because of parental difficulty, to assume a care-giving position with one or both parents. Abandonment coexists with excessive closeness (Sargent & Liebman, 1985). Each family has been challenged by a significant stress—moving, a serious accident, parental divorce, or the young woman's anorexia—and attempts to change too fast, leaving all family members with a sense of personal isolation and an awareness of mutual dependence. Fluctuations between attempts at extreme change and stasis leave the family out of control and without direction (Dym, 1985).

There are also marked dissimilarities in these four situations. The young women with anorexia differ in their ages, duration of weight loss, medical condition, and life experiences. Michelle has been losing weight only for 6 months and is not in serious difficulty, while Martha, only 2 years older and living at home, has been underweight for a longer period of time and is desperately ill as a result of her vomiting and extreme weight loss. Both Jennifer and Erica have been able to live away from home and look after themselves to some degree. Furthermore, there are significant differences in the responsiveness of the parents to external direction and to their daughters' strengths and their anorexia. This heterogeneity of developmental capacity, psychosocial skill, and achievement of the individual with the eating disorder and the marked differences in the family's ability to resolve conflicts, to maintain involvement, and to work together demand individualized treatment and a therapeutic approach that is sufficiently flexible to be used in various situations with caring, compassion, and respect.

AN OVERVIEW OF TREATMENT

Therapy for anorexia nervosa involves the creation of a new system, a therapeutic system that includes important family members and the therapist. Recognizing each family member's vulnerability, pain, and difficulty, the therapist must assume an active and highly responsive role within this system. The therapist must also appreciate the tenuous nature of family relationships, and the hurt and disappointment that these relationships have caused. The therapist further must establish a relationship with each family member that takes into account that individual's strength, caring, and passion. Like the hub of a wheel, the therapist becomes the central focus of treatment, building spokes to each family member before stressing the fragile connections between them. The therapist must also recognize that the family members may be unable to help each other at the beginning of treatment. The therapist's rules for participation, mutual respect, and individual well-being guide the initial phase of treatment.

As a team, the therapist and family collaborate on setting goals and achieving them, gradually developing continuity, consistency, and momentum. The creation of this team is the therapist's first and most important task, and it requires the therapist's professionalism, experience, confidence in his or her ability to treat anorexia, and a belief that all family members can live more successfully and more flexibly, both together and apart.

When the therapist meets the family, personal vulnerability and a lack of expressiveness and assertiveness with family relationships have fostered mutual disappointment and antagonism. This lack of interpersonal trust among family members, coupled with a powerful sense of responsibility for one another, leads to their continuing attempts to control one another. These attempts fail to achieve either change or personal validation, leaving everyone desperately frustrated and simultaneously isolated and overly tied together (Sargent & Liebman, 1985).

The anorexia itself involves (1) the achievement of personal control through refusal and self-denial and (2) the steadfast maintenance of involvement and interconnectedness through immaturity and incapacity. Although individual achievements are sought to create greater mutual respect and attention within the family, the end result of such achievements in a family that finds no meaning or solace in them is further isolation, loneliness, and emptiness. It is the therapist's task to develop successful interpersonal connections among family members and to provide validation for family members. In order to accomplish this, the therapist encourages a simultaneous focus on the people within the family and the importance of their cooperation in treatment. This permits the therapy to create unified wholes from the seemingly contradictory ambivalences—mind and body, being and doing, youth and age, rebellion and acceptance, separation and connectedness, male and female, vulnerability and strength—so prevalent in the families of young people with anorexia.

The course of treatment can be divided into stages. In the initial phase, the therapist uses metaphor, analogy, and explorations of complementarity to help the family appreciate the involvement of all family members in the problem and its solution. The therapist then assesses the family structure, the degree of individual differentiation of family members, and the developmental challenges of the position in the family life cycle. This initial assessment must take into account the needs of individual members, as well as those of the family as a whole.

The more difficulty the young person with anorexia has with self-preservation, self-respect, and self-care, the more the parents must establish control through rules and consistent expectations of the anorectic's behavior. As the young person is increasingly able to maintain her weight, initially above the lower limit of medical safety and subsequently in a healthy range, and to modulate and control her mood and impulsiveness, the parents can be assisted to become collaborators who encourage and reinforce independent action and expression. Gradually, depending on the young person's age, living circumstances, and ability to care for herself, the parents need to diminish their control, providing direction or support by stimulating further growth, self-reliance, and responsible self-care.

As issues concerning the young person's weight, eating habits, moods, and independence are discussed, the therapist develops themes of trust, availability, and mutual respect among family members. The therapist bases expectations concerning weight gain and physical recovery on the young person's age, the chronicity of the problems, and her anxiety about weight gain. The younger the individual with anorexia, the shorter the duration of symptoms, the less severe the weight loss, the more the therapist can expect consistent weight gain with recovery to normal weight over a relatively short period of time. The more chronic the weight loss, the more fearful the young person about weight gain, the more the therapist must be patient and anticipate a slow but steady weight gain over a more prolonged period of time. The therapist must be flexible in approaching each family and committed primarily to building trust among family members, as well as between family members and the therapist.

The second phase of treatment involves the restoration of effective, caring, and mutually satisfying relationships within the family. It is one thing for the parents to forego their differences and work together to help their starving daughter; it is quite another for them to begin to resolve differences and forgive disappointments that have been several years in creation. The chronicity of the anorexia itself seems to add to the disappointment and distrust that already exist within the family. The more chronic the anorexia, the more difficult the repair of relationships between mother and daughter, father and daughter, and husband and wife. This phase of therapy requires special delicacy and patience from the therapist.

Both parents ultimately learn to accept the disappointments of their adulthood and recognize the need to move on in their own lives while increasingly differentiating from their family of origin (White, 1983). In some cases, the parents may be separated already or may decide to separate. The therapist must limit the mutual blaming and help each parent begin to acknowledge his or her own role in the failures and disappointments of the marriage and the problems of parenting their anorectic daughter. Self-acceptance, forgiveness, assertiveness, and redirection of their own lives with renewed energy are important for both parents in this phase of therapy.

Each parent works on these issues in family sessions, parents only sessions, and individual sessions. The therapist can then lay the groundwork for each parent to develop a more satisfying relationship with the daughter. The mother can begin to see herself as a role model, guiding her daughter into adulthood. Competition between mother and daughter can be limited while the daughter learns to develop her own strength and the mother learns to encourage her daughter to become more independent, more self-reliant, and as accomplished as she can be. As the father recognizes the depth of his feeling for his daughter, he can help her appreciate both his respect for her strength and his tenderness toward her femininity. Throughout this process, the daughter learns to accept her sexuality rather than to see it as threatening or uncontrollable. The success of this phase of treatment depends heavily on the therapist's warmth, expression of affect, and appreciation of the disappointment and rage that involves at least three generations. The therapist also relies upon a sense of humor and an ability to introduce playfulness, teasing, and enjoyment of the moment into a family fraught with seriousness, intensity, and denial.

In this phase of the treatment, sessions are highly flexible. They may include the therapist and the anorectic without her siblings, with her siblings, with a boyfriend or friends; the therapist and the entire family; or the therapist and individual family members. The resulting picture of the family's connections with the community and the extended family allows the therapist to reinforce differentiation and connectedness simultaneously. Ultimately, the connectedness that develops is mutually reinforced among family members and is modulated by individual expression and assertiveness, as well as by the need for resolution of conflicts and negotiation of differences. Treatment then transforms fluctuations between no change and too much change into a steady, continuous process of change for the entire family as a unit and for its members as individuals.

The final phase of treatment involves the gradual disengagement of the therapist from the treatment system. The therapist may reduce the number of meetings with certain individuals, while maintaining a specific goal-directed relationship with one or more others. The therapist remains available to the family and its individual members over a long period of time, however, ready to assist individuals, pairs, or the family as a whole with future difficulties that may or may not be related to the anorexia.

CASE EXAMPLES

Michelle: Family Therapy with Subsequent Individual Therapy

Michelle came to treatment early in the course of her weight loss. Her parents were shaken by the possibility that she had a serious problem and, although tense, they were respectful, cooperative, and interested in both the therapist and the treatment. It was clear that her father had struggled throughout his adulthood to make an accommodation to his handicap that allowed him to see himself as an active, contributing member of his family and as a strong and powerful man. He had a tendency, initially, to be abrupt and critical of his daughters and of his wife. He became more critical when he felt threatened or incapable. Michelle's mother was an exceptionally bright, talented, and accomplished woman. She was successful in the business world, but she wondered if she had left mothering too quickly and was afraid that she would not be able to be simultaneously businesswoman, wife, and mother. Because of her fears, she had withdrawn from her husband and failed to recognize that she was already an excellent role model for her daughters. Despite these vulnerabilities, both parents had been successful enough in their professional and family lives to be able to approach Michelle's problem with a sense of openness and willingness to learn and resolve her difficulty. The affection of both parents for both daughters was apparent to the therapist in the first meeting.

Michelle herself was quiet and withdrawn. She had great difficulty expressing herself, but was able to appreciate the therapist's concern that she had somehow become the younger daughter in the family, switching positions with her sister. The therapist's initial approach was first to recognize, identify, and support the strengths of all four family members and to highlight the developmental and educational aspects of treatment, emphasizing that everyone was expected to be learning and no one individual was to be blamed for the fact that the family was in trouble. Circumstances, such as adolescence, cultural pursuit of thinness for women, and the recent family move to a competitive and somewhat "clickish" suburban community, were identified as the sources of the family's difficulty.

The therapist then focused on helping the parents to work together to expect that Michelle would gain weight steadily until she reached a normal weight, begin to express herself more freely, make friends, and develop a more assertive relationship with her sister. It became apparent that Michelle's father was sometimes overly harsh and that Michelle's mother was sometimes overly demanding and protective. The therapist helped the parents to become more accepting of the importance that each of them held for Michelle and to understand that each had things to teach her and ways to help her.

The overall progression of therapy followed the outline of the application of structural family therapy techniques to the treatment of early adolescent anorexia nervosa described by Minuchin, Rosman, and Baker (1978) and Sargent, Liebman, and Silver (1984). Michelle's weight gain was consistent and reflected the increased attention she received from both her parents, the respect of the therapist, and the acceptance of her sister. Michelle gradually became more assertive, less shy, and more expressive. After approximately 3½ months, she developed friendships and began to participate in sports and school activities. Therapy was discontinued with Michelle's weight at 110 pounds, 5 months after the family entered treatment.

The story, however, was not over. One year later, Michelle called the therapist herself, asking to talk about worries that she had in regard to her friends and her family. The therapist asked her to obtain permission from her parents to come to a session by herself, which she did. In that session, she described her feelings that she was being rejected by the more popular young people in her class and that she was clumsy and socially inept. As she discussed these feelings, it became apparent that Michelle was worried about her father's handicaps and identified with his clumsiness and sense of isolation. Michelle was also deeply worried about her mother's use of alcohol when she was stressed about work or dissatisfied in the home. As Michelle spoke about these issues, she began increasingly to appreciate her difference from her parents and her satisfaction with herself. She had maintained a normal healthy weight, had begun dating, and was continuing to participate in school activities. The therapist met with Michelle for five sessions over the ensuing 3 months, and she was able to gain a better perspective on herself and her family.

Over the next 18 months, Michelle's mother, her father, and her sister all came to the therapist for a small number of individual sessions to discuss their concerns about the present and the future. Michelle's mother came for four sessions in which she talked about her involvement in her business, her sense of pride in herself, her sense of accomplishment, and her need for relaxation and comfort with her advancing age and the changes that were taking place in her family.

Five years after the beginning of therapy, Michelle entered college, had a boyfriend and a regular summer job, and had maintained her weight without further eating-related symptoms. Her parents were still married, and both parents were successful in their jobs and satisfied with family life. Michelle's younger sister was entering her senior year in high school as a recognized leader among her peers with a clear sense of her own goals and direction.

Martha: Individual Therapy with Subsequent Family Therapy

Two compelling circumstances determined the treatment for Martha and her family. First, Martha was desperately ill and close to death. She required hospitalization for metabolic restoration and needed to begin to eat in a consistent fashion that would induce a slow, but steady, weight gain. Second, the level of antagonism, distrust, and vulnerability in her parents also required immediate attention. The therapist began treatment by ensuring that Martha was monitored physically. Both parents agreed to Martha's hospitalization and to a consistent daily food intake for her. The therapist participated in this by offering his ideas and suggestions to those of the parents so that the amount of food prescribed was neither too much nor too little and so that the amount of weight gain expected could be accomplished.

At the same time, the therapist worked diligently to develop a relationship with each parent in which each felt supported and validated. In individual sessions, the therapist consistently ratified the reality of their divorce and encouraged them to discuss their contributions to the divorce and to appreciate the strength of their affection for their children, including Martha, and their aspirations as parents and independent adults. Martha's mother needed help to accept her move away from her husband and her children, to forgive herself for her inability to make her marriage work, and to perceive her role as non-custodial parent as worthwhile and acceptable. Martha's father needed help to recognize his tendency to attempt to control those he loved and to learn to engender trust and respect in his relationships with his children.

The therapist's willingness to enter into supportive relationships with each parent before expecting them to work together created a renewed sense of hope among the entire family, including the siblings, the father's new wife, and the mother's boyfriend. The mutually respectful relationships that each developed with the therapist became a way of linking the parents together to provide support for Martha's growth, development, and recovery, while diminishing the resentments based on the failure of their marriage.

The therapist had ensured Martha's safety in the hospital in a way that did not demand too much of either parent and yet included them as active participants in her treatment. Martha gained weight steadily in the hospital, reaching a weight of 85 pounds, and was discharged after 6 weeks. She remained withdrawn and unassertive, however, and she was frightened by her weight gain, as well as by the possibility that one or both of her parents would abandon her after discharge.

The therapist continued with the family in outpatient treatment, meeting at times with the entire group and at times with the father, the stepmother and the children or the mother, the boyfriend, and the children. He helped the parents to encourage Martha's participation in school and peer activities and to recognize her position as a peer among her siblings. Both parents patiently made themselves available and offered Martha their support as she continued to gain weight and gradually controlled her tendency to binge and vomit.

One year after the beginning of treatment, Martha was at a normal weight, bingeing and vomiting less than once a week, attending school regularly, and beginning to participate in peer activities. Martha's father and mother talked infrequently, but cordially, and were able to discuss concerns about their children in a mutually supportive and collaborative way. Martha's mother had remarried and obtained a better job. Martha's father and stepmother had a new baby who was successfully integrated into the family without a recurrence of Martha's symptoms.

Jennifer: Simultaneous Individual and Family Therapy

Jennifer required the therapist's support of her as a college student who lived away from home and was responsible for her academic life and her own therapy. At the same time, it was necessary to ratify her connection to her parents, validating their concern for her and her need to be sure that her parents were safe at home. The therapist had simultaneously to develop a relationship with Jennifer and a relationship with her entire family.

Family sessions were held on a monthly basis. The parents traveled to Jennifer's college and learned from her of her needs for support and understanding. They expressed their expectation that she keep herself healthy, gradually gain weight, and control her eating-related symptoms. All agreed that Jennifer would look to her therapist rather than to her parents for support and guidance about her relationship with her boyfriend, her school performance, and her living situation. Jennifer's parents agreed that their role was to be available and understanding, but not to be controlling or excessively demanding. Gradually, each parent was able to talk with Jennifer about his or her independent relationship with her and to reassure her that they were looking after their own lives. Sometimes the parents saw their own therapist at home to discuss their marriage, their feelings about their daughters, and their individual sense of direction in their lives. The theme of abandonment and the need for Jennifer and her parents to be available to each other recurred repeatedly throughout the first year of treatment.

During weekly sessions with Jennifer, the therapist increasingly challenged her to be expressive, assertive, and accepting of herself. She gradually recognized her hunger for accomplishment, her desire to be loved, and her attractiveness, as well as her pleasure in physical closeness with her boyfriend. Jennifer slowly came to understand her need to develop her own goals and set her own standards of accomplishment. Jennifer also needed to learn to accept her moodiness, her frustration with herself, and her drive to be successful as she began to live her life as a college student and to plan her life as an adult.

The therapist's involvement with Jennifer's parents diminished gradually as Jennifer reported successful visits home, an increased sense of comfort with her family, and an increased ability to have privacy in her parents' home and to participate actively in family gatherings. Jennifer obtained her parents' support to drop out of college and to re-enter school after a successful job experience. She learned to acknowledge and accept her lack of control at the time of the automobile accident that had immediately preceded her weight loss. She also managed her own apartment, decided to live with her boyfriend, and learned to accept the uncertainty in their relationship.

The therapist was not only Jennifer's trusted ally, but also someone who knew her family and appreciated both the strengths and the weaknesses of her parents. Jennifer needed help to negotiate the transition from daughter to young adult while maintaining a connection with her parents and remaining suppor-

tive of them as they increasingly recognized and ratified her maturity. Three years after the beginning of treatment, Jennifer graduated from college and obtained a highly competitive position in a firm in another city. She moved, but maintained her relationship with her boyfriend and has contacted the therapist intermittently. Her weight was normal, and she was able to eat without much difficulty most of the time. At times, she became dissatisfied with her body, and she occasionally engaged in bingeing and purging when stressed. She was visiting her family for holidays and talking with them whenever she and/or they wished.

Erica: Individual Therapy with Family Support

Erica presented the therapist with several challenges. She wanted individual therapy and was strongly opposed to the participation of her parents in her treatment. She was also quite erratic, impulsive, and dangerously ill. Individual therapy was explained to Erica as an experiment to see if she could keep her weight above a safe minimum, keep her twice weekly appointments on her own, and pay for treatment herself, or whether she would need family help in her treatment.

Erica had been quite successful during adolescence and in college, and she had been able to live and support herself in a foreign country. The therapist noted these accomplishments, indicating his acceptance of her, and she was able to respond by being consistent and responsible in her treatment. In return, the therapist resisted the intrusions of her family, although he contacted them and assured them that her health was being monitored and that he would inform them if Erica was not taking care of herself or coming for sessions. Only when Erica was convinced that the therapist was more interested in her than in her powerful and well-known parents was she able gradually to see her need for her parents' support, recognition, and acceptance.

Erica had been her mother's mother, and she had been the link between her divorced, but warring, parents. Erica wanted to bridge the gap between herself and her parents in her own way, at her own speed, but her parents had expected too much accomplishment or too much responsiveness to their needs. As she became involved in a relationship with the therapist, who maintained contact with each of her parents, she diminished her role in their lives. She began to trust the therapist's appreciation of her strength and find that strength in herself.

Over 2 years, Erica learned to accept the therapist's warmth and respect, and to use her strength, her vibrancy, and her determination to find her own place in life, regardless of how famous her name or how powerful her parents. When she felt strong and physically healthy enough, Erica invited her parents separately to sessions to ask for what she needed from them in words rather than to engender their involvement through vulnerability and sickness. She was able to grieve for the loss of the aunt who had mothered her when her own mother could not and to appreciate her own sexuality and vibrancy. Like many other young women with anorexia, Erica had used her sexuality to connect herself with stronger men who would look after her, but made her feel dominated. As she began to recognize the possibility of choice and enjoyment in relationships and in her body, she was increasingly able to see herself as an adult woman separate from her mother and independent of her father. Three years after the beginning of treatment, Erica was at a normal weight, was in control of her impulses, did not abuse drugs or alcohol, and was working steadily. She was gradually beginning to date men for social contact, mutuality, and enjoyment.

REFERENCES

Dym, B. (1985). Eating disorders and the family: A model for intervention. In S.W. Emmett (Ed.), *Theory and treatment of anorexia nervosa and bulimia* (pp. 174–193). New York: Brunner/ Mazel.

Minuchin, S., Rosman, B., & Baker, L. (1978). *Psychosomatic families: Anorexia nervosa in context*. Cambridge, MA: Harvard University Press.

Sargent, J., & Liebman, R. (1985). Eating disorders. In S. Henao & N. Grose (Eds.), *Principles of family systems in family medicine* (pp. 213–242). New York: Brunner/Mazel.

Sargent, J., Liebman, R., & Silver, M. (1984). Family therapy for anorexia. In D.M. Garner & P. Garfinkel (Eds.), *Treatment of anorexia nervosa and bulimia* (pp. 257–279). New York: Guilford Press.

White, M. (1983). Anorexia nervosa: A transgenerational system perspective. *Family Process*, *22*(3), 255–273.

10

Anorexia Nervosa: A Cybernetic Perspective

Michael White, BASW
Family and Marital Therapist
Visiting Consultant, Glenside Hospital
Dulwich, South Australia

I INTRODUCED MYSELF TO SUSAN and her parents in the waiting room. It was immediately obvious that Susan had anorexia nervosa. She was extremely thin and suffering from hypothermia, wearing more clothes than the weather would normally have necessitated. I walked alongside Susan to my room, sensing her apprehension. Upon arrival, when seated, I asked her to tell me about herself. She somewhat reluctantly informed me that she was 16 years of age, had suffered from anorexia nervosa for 2 years, and that everyone thought she was thin but that she did not agree. Her parents, Tom and Carol, then introduced themselves. They said the situation was urgent and that, despite a recent hospitalization, Susan's weight was decreasing quickly. She now weighed 32 kg and still exercised at every opportunity. She had developed sores on her back from her rigourous programme of sit-ups. Carol and Tom feared for her life. They were understandably feeling desperate and impotent.

I asked Susan and her parents what they thought had caused the problem. Tom and Carol replied that they were still entirely confused as to what it was all about. Susan had not previously given them any cause for concern, and they had been shocked by the sudden onset of the symptoms. Turning to Susan, I asked if she was able to explain how it was that she was experiencing a life-threatening condition but was unable to appreciate this fact. She replied that she could not. She then said that she thought she was fat and that she was scared her eating would go out of control if she tried to put on weight. I asked if she felt guilty about eating and she gave an affirmative answer. At this point Carol interjected, telling Susan that her fear was groundless and pleading with her to see that it was destroying her life.

Without warning, Susan's anger flashed. She attacked Carol for "always picking," charging that it was Carol's fault that she felt so miserable. Tom interrupted with "Now Susan, I think. . . ." Before he could complete his sentence Susan turned her fury on him. Then, just as suddenly, she was in tears, expressing remorse. She told Carol and Tom how sorry she was for causing them so many problems and for hurting them so much. Between sobs, Susan said that it must be very difficult for them to have a daughter like her and that they did not really deserve all this trouble.

Susan's tears subsided and she withdrew. I asked her how she was feeling and she said "terrible." Was the feeling she was experiencing like guilt? She said that it was. I wondered aloud if at these times Susan felt like disappearing, like erasing herself as a person. Susan replied, "Yes, I feel all wrong."

Turning to Carol and Tom I said it was my experience that, although parents develop their own private explanations about the cause of anorexia nervosa, they were usually very reluctant to disclose these thoughts. I told them that I had even come across mothers who wholly and secretly blamed themselves for

their daughter's problem, swallowing the distorted view that has so often appeared in popular and professional literature that anorexia nervosa is caused by intrusive and overbearing mothers. Carol immediately burst into tears and was unable to speak for some minutes. When she had regained some composure, she said that she had "always believed, no not believed, had always known" that she was to blame. I invited Carol to help me understand how she had coped over the past two years with her despair and this burden of guilt, how she had been able to endure the loneliness that had accompanied those secret thoughts. Had she felt like she was disappearing? Had she also wanted to become invisible?

Carol was tearful again, giving me details of her experience, telling me that she had been angry at times, and that although she knew that it was wrong for her to encourage Susan to eat she just couldn't stop herself from doing so. I said that I would like to be able to appreciate more of her experience of the past two years.

At this point, Susan looked volcanic. Noticing this, Tom attempted to cool the situation with a rational discussion of his and Carol's experience, vaguely alluding to some of their possible failures as parents and rounding off with a plea for Susan to show more consideration to Carol. Then, the cycle repeated itself with Susan experiencing anger and then self-recrimination, with Tom fading away, feeling ineffectual, and with Carol distressed and defensive.

THE SEARCH FOR A SOLUTION

Therapists who have worked with families that have a daughter with anorexia nervosa will be familiar with the "guilt/blame" cycles that feature in the above example of family interaction. These cycles are repetitive. They are cycles in which each member interacts in relation to certain beliefs or premises about the problem that inspire attempted solutions that do not bring relief. Family members "just go round and round in terms of the old premises" (Bateson, 1972, p. 427).

These premises establish a dormitive construction[1] of the problem, a construction in which the problem is explained in terms of personal inadequacy, incompetence, imperfection and disloyalty. The failure of the attempted solutions, solutions that require more "correct" and more loyal behavior, serves to reinforce these premises. Family members, trapped in this "web of belief," appear unable to respond to each other differently. Evans-Pritchard vividly portrays the consequences of such a web of belief in his analysis of the belief system of the Azande tribe:

> In this web of belief every strand depends upon every other strand and a Zande cannot get out of its meshes because it is the only world he knows. The web is not an external structure in which he is enclosed. It is the texture of his thought, and he cannot think that his thought is wrong. (1937, pp. 194–195)

Thus, family members are restrained in the search for and application of alternative solutions. They experience that everything is so wrong, that they are personally wrong despite their hard work to avoid being wrong. In response, "to disappear" presents as a particularly viable solution. From this perspective, the symptoms of anorexia nervosa can be considered the symptoms of a disappearance.

In an earlier paper I discussed the therapeutic implications of considering anorexia nervosa within the context of the family's system of rigid and implicit beliefs (White, 1983).[2] I suggested that certain aspects of this system of beliefs established a vulnerability in certain daughters for anorexia nervosa, a vulnerability often activated by societal pressure for idealized body images for women.

In this paper I intend to broaden and extend the analysis of the context of anorexia nervosa by applying certain propositions from cybernetic theory. I will also discuss the therapeutic implications of these propositions.

CYBERNETIC THEORY

Cybernetic theory provides a metaphor for the analysis of events or interaction within systems. This metaphor is regularly employed by family therapists for the consideration of problems in context

---

[1]All explanations that propose some internal quality or quantity, or lack of the same, as casual, are, according to Bateson (1972), dormative explanations that put to sleep our "critical facility."

> Relationship is not internal to the single person. It is nonsense to talk about "dependency" or "aggressiveness" or "pride" and so on. All such words have their roots in what happens between persons, not in some something-or-other inside the person. (1980, p. 147)

[2]For a second description of this context see "Reconstructing the Family's Reality—The Struggle of a Young Anorectic Woman and Her Family's Way of Viewing the World." (Durrant, 1984)

and for the derivation of and application of appropriate interventions. Gregory Bateson's explication of cybernetic theory (Bateson, 1972, 1980) is the one most frequently referred to by family therapists and has provided the basis for important innovation.[3] This theory contains various interrelated propositions, some of which will be discussed in relation to anorexia nervosa and its treatment. I have also discussed these propositions and implications elsewhere (White, 1986).

Negative Explanation

> We consider what alternative possibilities could conceivably have occurred and then ask why many of these alternatives were not followed, so that the particular event was one of those few that would, in fact, occur. (Bateson, 1972, p. 399)

Cybernetic theory establishes a negative explanation of events in systems. Negative explanation requires that all such events be examined with reference to restraint. It proposes that events take their course because they are restrained in relation to alternative courses.

The application of cybernetic theory to events in families establishes a line of enquiry into those events that is in marked contrast to the line of enquiry informed by positive explanation. Positive explanation proposes that events take their course because they are driven or propelled in that direction, invoking notions of quantities, of forces and impacts. These are dormitive notions that, when applied to living systems, promote an explanation of and investigation of events in terms of motivation, drive, impulse and other "internal" qualities.

Negative explanation raises questions as to why the particular event, for example, the development of the problem or the solution attempted by a family member, was "one of those few that would, in fact, occur." This line of enquiry establishes a curiosity as to what has restrained family members from participating in alternate interactions, from discovering alternate solutions.

In the consideration of anorexia nervosa and the attempted solutions of family members to this problem, those various alternative directions in life so constructed as "making an appearance," "turning on to independence," "self-realizing," "becoming ones own person," and "maturing" are alternatives that appear unavailable or untenable. Thus, the line of enquiry is shaped by an investigation into what has restrained family members from participating in these alternative possibilities. This line of enquiry can be introduced at the outset of therapy by the introduction of cybernetic questions.[4] I have included a sample of such questions here. These questions can be asked of all family members.

- From a consideration of recent events, it is now evident to us all that every day there is less of you, physically as you lose weight and mentally as you

---

[3]For example see "Hypothesizing-Circularity-Neutrality: Three Guidelines for the Conductor of the Session." (Palazzoli, et al. 1980)

[4]The practice of formulating questions that intorduce an appreciation of "circularity" and "recursiveness" in systems is well established. For example, see Palazzoli, et al. (1980) and Tomm (1986).

become more taken over by a preoccupation with food and weight loss. What is it that would so confine a young woman to a "self-erasing" course and exclude her from a "self-embracing" direction in life?

- I believe that we all share a similar interest in what could have confined you to a "disappearance" at the very stage in your development that you were about to make a stronger appearance. What ideas do you have about why you haven't experienced an entitlement to try other directions in life to see how they fit for you?

- We can all be very curious about why a young woman of your age is restricted to "invisibility" when others of your age feel entitled to greater visibility in every way. Can we discuss this together in an attempt to make sense of this puzzle?

I have termed these "cybernetic questions" as they require that family members derive a negative explanation of anorexia nervosa, an explanation at variance with their dormitive and problem-perpetuating construction of events. This line of enquiry readies the therapeutic system for more specific speculation about restraints.

Restraint

When discussing negative explanation, Bateson postulates several categories of restraint. These include restraints relating to (1) the economics of energy, (2) the economics of alternatives, (3) feedback, and (4) redundancy

(1972, p. 403). I will restrict my discussion to restraints of redundancy and restraints of feedback.

Redundancy

> My image is my aggregation and organization of information about the perceived object, aggregated and integrated according to rules of which I am totally unconscious. I can . . . know about these rules; but I cannot be conscious of the process of their working. (Bateson, 1978, p. 237)

Restraints of redundancy include the network of presuppositions, premises and expectations that make up a person's map of the world. Bateson has variously referred to this network as "fundamentals," "matrix," "surface," or "hard programmed ideas." All description and explanation of events is derived by the mapping of incoming data (news of difference) onto this network. The data are tried against the network, and only data that fit some regularity or pattern have meaning to the recipient. In this sense, redundancy is a synonym for pattern or meaning, occurring when we have "information here about something there" (Bateson, 1978, p. 210), when we are able, from a part of the total information, to predict wholes out "there." Thus, restraints of redundancy establish rules for the selection of information about the perceived object or event. In this way, restraints establish sensory limitations.

In discussing restraints of redundancy that select out "anorectic responses," I will refer separately to the societal context and the context of the family's rigid system of implicit belief. I acknowledge that many aspects of this division are false as both contexts participate in and reflect the ideology of patriarchy.[5]

1. Societal Context. Gender stereotyping is established by various premises that act as restraints. According to these, a woman can only be valued by others and by herself according to specific and limited criteria. These premises reinforce each other and here I will mention just a few.

One such premise is that if a woman is to be appreciated then she should be self-denying and dependent. Behavior that fits this pattern includes subjugation to the authority of men; the surrender of authority in relation to personal knowledges or in relation to her own experience. Emotional fulfillment is to be achieved by behaviours patterned on the nurturing of and caring for others. Those personal desires that are expressed should be expressed indirectly.[6]

Another premise is that for a woman to experience worthiness she must conform to the significant trend of the last 20 years toward an "ideal" of thinness (Garner and Garfinkel, 1984). According to this premise, a woman's experience of worthiness is contingent upon how perfectly she can replicate the established ideal. This ideal is reinforced daily in a thousand different ways. For example, in my city there was recently a billboard advertising campaign for women's briefs. The billboard pictured young and

very thin women wearing only briefs and the caption ran "The Perfect Shape." I have no doubt that, apart from the effects of conscious scanning, such advertising provides a very strong subliminal reinforcement of the "ideal."

A third premise is that if a woman is to contribute then she should preoccupy herself with providing the correct food for others, particularly for members of her family. Media advertising plays a highly significant part in this as it directs most of its indoctrination about food to women. A recent example was an advertisement on television for a particular brand of margarine. It depicted a mother succeeding in making an acceptable contribution by purchasing the right margarine for her husband and children. The jingle ran- "You Ought to be Congratulated." This premise is also reinforced daily in a thousand different ways.

Premises that measure a woman's value by her ability to be self-denying, dependent, indirect, thin, and preoccupied with food provides a context for the selection of anorectic behaviour. An insidious paradox is generated, one that is repeatedly reinforced in various ways: "discover yourself through losing yourself" and "find yourself by disappearing." This easily translates into "self-actualise through anorexia nervosa" and "arrive in life the anorectic way." Behaviour that does not fit with these premises has no meaning in the receiving

---

[5]Due to space considerations, the discussion of this context will be cursory. There is considerable literature that provides an analysis of this context. For example, for discussion of the history of the subjugation of women's knowledge see Spender (1983) and Rich (1977). For discussion of the relationship of "ideal" body image for women to patriarchy see Orbach (1978) and Chernin (1981).

[6]The behaviour of women with anorexia nervosa is often considered "manipulative." This term is used in a perjorative and dormitive sense. In view of the context of anorexia nervosa, it is more reasonable to consider this behavior as "indirect."

context and cannot be appreciated; that is, such behaviour cannot be selected out for survival.

This analysis of restraints brings specificity to cybernetic questions. The following questions provide a small sample of the options available. These questions are prefaced by the more general questions that have already introduced, to family members, a cybernetic construction of anorexia nervosa:

- Are you familiar with any examples of the idea that women should "be for others" rather than "be for themselves?" How do you think these examples could support a self-erasing lifestyle for women?
- How could this history of the subjugation of women's knowledge influence a woman to rub out her own opinion? How could this exclude her appearance in life?
- If the media successfully deceives a woman into believing she is only making a contribution when she is preoccupied with food and weight, and only worthy when conforming to an artificial "perfect shape," how could this state of deception make it difficult for that woman to experience an entitlement to her own course in life?
- If a woman were to succeed in achieving this impoverishing "perfect shape," do you think it would be more or less possible for her to appreciate herself?
- How do you think a pursuit of thinness and a pursuit of invisibility are related? How do these pursuits render women's visibility untenable?
- What specific options in life would be unavailable to a woman who was

indoctrinated with the idea that she must "discover herself by losing herself?" How do you think this indoctrination would make it difficult for a young woman to claim herself?

2. Family Context. Although all women are subject to the above-mentioned premises that promote impoverishing gender stereotyping, only a small percentage of them develop anorexia nervosa. What renders some women more vulnerable than others? Previously I argued that the family's rigid system of implicit beliefs provides the context for the creation of this vulnerability (White, 1983). I proposed that these beliefs were transgenerational in nature and included (a) a high value on the loyalty of family members to each other and to family tradition, (b) a specific role prescription for a daughter in which her value is measured according to the extent of "being for otherness" that she displays, and (c) a strong emphasis on dormitive terms of explanation and description. Guilt is the prescribed "felt" experience for a daughter who does not meet these criteria.

The proposal that aspects of the family's rigid system of implicit beliefs provides a context that establishes a vulnerability for anorexia nervosa in certain daughters brings further specificity to the cybernetic questions. Before introducing these questions the therapist suggests that it could be productive to establish an enquiry into how some young women are more vulnerable than others to a self-denying, dependent and empty lifestyle.

- Do you think that those women in your family who have been more preoccupied with "being for others" than with "being for themselves" would be more confined to a self-erasing lifestyle and experience less entitlement to a more self-embracing course?

- In what ways do you imagine that a specialization in loyalty and devotion would restrict a woman to a course of favouring others rather than self-promotion?

- In reviewing this strong history of certain daughters surrendering themselves to the dictates of guilt, how do you think the strength of this inherited history counters the development of your own history-making direction?

- How do the aspects of this tradition of loyalty that we have discovered establish an indebtedness to the past, and how does your membership of past generations interrupt any experience of entitlement to your own future?

Similar questions can be constructed regarding the restraints operating on other family members in relation to their habitual and problem perpetuating attempted solutions.

Feedback

> . . . the family is a cybernetic system . . . and usually when systemic pathology occurs, the members blame each other, or sometimes themselves. But the truth of the matter is that both these alternatives are fundamentally arrogant. Either alternative assumes that the individual human being has total power over the system of which he or she is part (Bateson, 1972, p. 438).

According to Bateson, circularity is a fundamental phenomenon of all systems; "events at any position in the circuit may be expected to have effect at *all* positions on the circuit at later times" (Bateson, 1972, p. 404). Circularity proposes a recursiveness in all systems, where events feed back on themselves. Recursive circuits "generate a non-random response to a random event at that position in the circuit at which the random event occurred" (Bateson, 1972, p. 404). From this explication the concept of feedback is derived; feedback as restraint. This suggests that (1) any enduring changes in a part of a system must be complementary to changes in the larger system, and that (2) such changes are not random, but both directional and relational.

Bateson was first alerted to the phenomenon of feedback by his observation of directional change in his field-work with the Iatmul tribe in New Guinea (Bateson, 1978). Through this observation, Bateson, already dissatisfied with the "unipolar psychological words" (1978, p. 47) that were a description for only one end of a relationship, began to think about and develop classifications of processes.

In contrast to Weiner, who associated cybernetics with control, Bateson used the term cybernetics to describe complete circuiting systems (Bateson, 1978, p. 52). Bateson believed the introduction of the term *control* to be unfortunate in that it established a propensity to select out the wrong unit in the analysis of events. He argued that this idea suggested that a part can control the whole and implied an artificial boundary between parts, provoking a failure to recognize interlocking processes in "thinking-and-acting" systems and leading to premises that pitted species against species and species against the environment—"an ecology of bad ideas" (Bateson, 1972, p. 484).

Bateson cited the selection of the wrong unit for examination as generative of dormitive explanation for events in systems. All descriptions of causes that invoke some characteristic within a person, such as, dependency or aggression, provide dormitive explanations. These terms have their origins in relationships between persons, and these relationships precede all such terms of description. Dormitive notions divert explanation away from the interactional context, and provoke a "very great nonsense, which only hides the real questions" (Bateson, 1980, p. 147).

In therapy, dormitive explanation can be challenged, and the "real questions" can be addressed if the therapist develops a formulation of the problem that emphasizes the double or multiple sides of nature of all description.

> We commonly speak as though a single 'thing' could 'have' some characteristic . . . that is how a language is made . . . but this way of thinking is not good enough in science or epistemology. To think straight, it is advisable to expect all qualities and attributes, adjectives, and so on to refer to at least two sets of interactions in time (Bateson, 1980, p. 67).

This emphasis assists the therapist to elaborate complementary descriptions of events in family interaction, descriptions that lead to the development of questions that require family members to shape two-sided descriptions of events. After the introduction of such questions, it becomes difficult for family members to describe events relating to the problem without invoking the concept of circularity.

Complementary Description and Complementary Questioning

Young women with anorexia nervosa appear to be surrendering responsibility for the supervision of their lives to others. They become more dependent over time and less authoritative in relation to their future, less able to put their weight behind their own hopes. As the preoccupation with food and weight increases, these women find it more difficult to identify their own opinion in relation to most matters. If freedom has to do with choice, these women experience increasing oppression as they become more "taken over" by those around them and by the symptoms of anorexia nervosa.

Correspondingly, those around the young woman, particularly the parents, specialize in super-responsibility for her life. Parents attempt to exercise their authority more strongly in relation to their daughter's future, putting more weight behind their hopes for their daughter. As the young woman becomes more preoccupied with food and weight others take over decision making in most areas of her life. Mothers are sometimes particularly vulnerable to participating with their daughters in this way because of their own subjugation to a "being for otherness" criterion.

This complementary description forms the basis of a line of enquiry that I term "complementary questioning." These questions require that family members derive two-sided and circular descriptions of events. Care is taken to ensure that family members understand that the mutual invitations for this complementary participation are issued inadvertently.

- As you put less weight behind your hopes, how does this invite your parents to put more weight behind their hopes for you? As your daughter puts less weight behind her own hopes, how does this invite you to put more weight behind your hopes for her?

- As you weigh less and become less influential, how do you weigh more heavily on the minds of your parents and invite them to become more influential in your life? As your daughter weighs less and becomes less influential in her life, how does this weigh more heavily on your minds and invite you to become more influential in her life?

- How does your disappearance in life invite others to make a stronger appearance in your life? How does your daughter's disappearance in life invite you to make a stronger appearance in her life?

- In what ways has your surrender placed your future in the hands of your parents? In what ways has your daughter's surrender placed her future in your hands?

- How does your emptiness invite your parents to participate more fully in your life? How does your daughter's emptiness invite you to participate more fully in her life?

- In what way does your dependency status invite your parents to pull more strings? In what way does your daughter's dependency status invite you to pull more strings for her?

Complementary questions that reverse this punctuation are also introduced:

- How does your vulnerability to guilt invite your daughter to give you responsibility for her life? How does

your parents' vulnerability to guilt invite you to give them more responsibility for your life?

READINESS AND THE ENDURANCE OF THE NEW

The introduction of a cybernetic perspective via this enquiry into restraints of redundancy and restraints of feedback establishes a new "code book" or receiving context that allows new ideas to be selected out within the therapeutic system. In contributing to the therapeutic system's readiness to select out the new for survival, cybernetic and complementary questions themselves provoke change.

Further, since cybernetic and complementary questions introduce an explanation of anorexia nervosa that is at variance with the family's established explanation, these questions establish conditions for double description, conditions that provide the source for all new responses.[7] Thus, alternative directions become available for family member participation. Cybernetic and complementary questions can also be utilized in other specific methods for establishing contexts for double description. As I have discussed these methods elsewhere (White, 1986), I will only briefly address them here.

Mapping Relative Influence

After mapping the influence of the problem in the lives of family members, the therapist formulates questions that require family members to map their influence in the life of the problem, to

[7]According to Bateson, conditions for double description allow distinctions to be drawn by the recipients, and these distinctions provide the source for all new responses.

select out "facts" which are at variance with their experience of the problem's oppression of them. These are facts that have not had any correspondence with regularities in the receiving context, and, thus, have not previously been selected out for survival by family members.

- In view of your restriction to a disappearing life-style, it is quite an achievement that you have kept alive some hope that you could have a future appearance and arrive at being your own person. How have you managed this?
- Because of your vulnerability to guilt, in what other ways could you have inadvertently invited your daughter to sell you responsibility for her life? In these examples, how have you managed to escape the dictates of guilt?
- Although you have been inviting others to pull the strings for you in various ways, you have not entirely exhausted the possibilities and achieved a puppet status. Perhaps we can discuss these possibilities and talk about how you have been able to avoid a complete takeover?
- Having discussed other ways that your daughter could have surrendered to the tradition of loyalty of daughters in your family, what do you think it is about her that enabled her to avoid being totally overwhelmed by guilt? What does this mean about future possibilities?

Collapsing Time

The therapist can collapse time on the participation of family members in the evolution of the disappearing life-style. This evolution is both directional and

relational. Collapsing time allows family members to draw distinctions around descriptions of participation at different points in time in this evolutionary process, distinctions that would otherwise be lost due to the phenomena of adaption and addiction.

- Should you side further with this state of deception, blind to your oppression, what hopes of being your own person would you have to dismiss?
- If you were to allow yourselves to be more overtaken by this tradition, in what ways do you think you would be more wholly involved in your daughter's life? How could this correspond to a more partial status for your daughter?
- If your daughter were to take her disappearance further, what other possibilities could be exhausted by her to invite others to pull the strings for her, possibilities that would invite you to make a weightier appearance in her life?
- Should you comply more with the family tradition for certain daughters to be for others and give themselves away, what aspects of the lives of women who have gone before you could you more fully replicate?

Raising Dilemmas

In raising a dilemma, the therapist assists in the drawing out of two elaborate and alternative descriptions of family member participation in relation to the problem. One of these descriptions details the steps required for further compliance with the restraints and for the furthering of complementary participation with anorexia nervosa. The other details what steps would be required to challenge the restraints and to defy this complementary participation around a disappearing lifestyle. These descriptions are stood side by side and comparison is invited. Dilemmas over participation in relation to anorexia nervosa can be organized around various themes of opposition. Questions can then be derived that promote a debate over readiness for change.

- Do you think you should resign yourself to instructions for a self-erasing course in life, or do you think that you are entitled to a more self-embracing direction?
- Do you think that you should submit to tradition and constrain yourself to an appearance in your daughter's life, or do you think that you have a right to put some of your weight behind directions that have more to do with favouring yourselves and your marriage?
- Do you believe your daughter should restrict herself to an indirect life and continue to invite others to pull her strings, or do you think that she has the right to be more direct and self-fulfilling?
- Do you think that you should apply yourself to a replication of the past or do you think that you should pioneer your own history-making direction in life?

Before the debate generated by these questions is settled, speculation about the consequences of change can be introduced via further questions:

- What taken for granted arrangements and values in our world would be disrupted if young women like your daughter experienced an entitlement to oppose women's subordination and to embrace their own power and competence?
- How do you think that your parents would cope if you refused to invite them to pull your strings? If they were invited to become less busy with you, what could they become busy with instead? What other hopes could they put their weight behind?
- What do you think would be the consequence to your family history if you embark on a history-making and self-embracing direction? How do you think you would cope with the guilt that you would experience upon claiming yourself?
- You will experience guilt when you take for yourself by eating and putting on weight because this has to do with defying a being for others lifestyle. When you do this, how do you think you could prevent guilt from driving you back to an empty direction?

Experiments and Responding to Responses

The debate over dilemmas establishes a readiness in family members to embark on experiments that favour new directions. Most of these experiments are spontaneous, the outcome of the receipt of news of difference, although they can be more explicitly planned. These experiments involve all family members in different ways and can range from direct action, for example, defacing "perfect shape" billboards, to steps to disrupt the complementary interaction around anorexia nervosa. As therapy enters the "middle stage," the therapist co-evolves with family members in the selection of and endurance of new responses. Here, the derivation of questions is also helpful.

- Now that you are history makers, that is, you have taken over the writing of your history from the writers of your old history, how has this history-making status changed your future from the future that had been assigned to you?

CONCLUSION

The foregoing discussion presented the analysis of anorexia nervosa in a context that I have found most helpful in the consideration of and treatment of this problem. This is a cybernetic analysis that emphasizes notions of restraint relating to redundancy and feedback. The therapeutic implications of this analysis were reviewed with a strong emphasis on the construction of the "real questions." I have argued that these questions establish a cybernetic appreciation of anorexia nervosa and have proposed that they provoke new responses from family members in that they provide conditions for double description and establish a new "code book" in the receiving context.

REFERENCES

Bateson, G. (1972). *Steps to an ecology of mind.* New York: Ballantine Books.

Bateson, G. (1978). The birth of a matrix or double bind and epistemology. In M. Berger (Ed.), *Beyond the double bind.* New York: Brunner/Mazel.

Bateson, G. (1980). *Mind and nature: A necessary unity.* New York: Bantam Books.

Evans-Pritchard, E. (1937). *Witchcraft, oracles and magic among the Azande.* Oxford: Clarendon Press.

Garner, D.M., & Garfinkel, D.E. (1984). *Handbook of psychotherapy for anorexia nervosa and bulimia.* New York: Guilford Press.

White, M. (1983). Anorexia nervosa: A transgenerational system perspective. *Family Process, 22*(3), 255–273.

White, M. (1986). Negative explanation, restraint and double description: A template for family therapy. *Family Process, 25*(2).

Index

FAMILY THERAPY COLLECTIONS

FORTHCOMING VOLUMES